THOMAS MERTON

when the trees say nothing

writings on nature

THOMAS MERTON

when the trees say nothing

edited by Kathleen Deignan
drawings by John Giuliani
with a foreword by Thomas Berry

 SORIN BOOKS   Notre Dame, IN

SORIN BOOKS is dedicated to providing resources to assist readers to enhance their quality of life. We welcome your comments and suggestions, which may be conveyed to:

SORIN BOOKS
P.O. Box 1006
Notre Dame, IN 46556-1006
Fax: 1-800-282-5681

The author and publisher gratefully acknowledge the following sources from which excerpts were compiled:

Run to the Mountain: The Journals of Thomas Merton, Volume One 1939–1941 by Thomas Merton and edited by Patrick Hart. Copyright © 1995 by The Merton Legacy Trust. Reprinted by permission of HarperCollins Publishers, Inc.

Entering the Silence: The Journals of Thomas Merton, Volume Two 1941–1952 by Thomas Merton and edited by Jonathan Montaldo. Copyright © 1995 by The Merton Legacy Trust. Reprinted by permission of HarperCollins Publishers, Inc.

The copyright acknowledgments are continued on page 191.

---

www.sorinbooks.com

International Standard Book Number: 1-893732-60-6

Cover design by Katherine Robinson Coleman

Text design by Brian C. Conley

Printed and bound in the United States of America.

Library of Congress Cataloging-in-Publication Data
    Merton, Thomas, 1915-1968.
When the trees say nothing : writings on nature / Thomas Merton ;
    edited with an introduction by Kathleen Deignan ; illustrated by John Giuliani.
        p. cm.
    ISBN 1-893732-60-6
    1. Nature--Religious aspects--Catholic Church. I. Deignan, Kathleen,
    1947- II. Title.
BX1795.N36 M47 2003
508--dc21

                                                    2002015094
                                                    CIP

For Ann Christian Deignan
beautiful epiphany of Earth's poetry and healing

For Vin Giuliani
whose soul speaks the language of silence

CONTENTS

ACKNOWLEDGMENTS

This book is the harvest of many seeds planted over decades by the women of the Congregation of Notre Dame who introduced me to the wisdom of Thomas Merton: Ellen McNamara, Eileen Fitzgerald, and especially Marie Schmidt, with whom I daily shared the joy of Merton's abiding presence during our time together. Father John Giuliani watered those seeds during our graced friendship beginning in 1968, as we labored to realize something of Merton's vision by founding the Thomas Merton House of Hospitality in Bridgeport, Connecticut, and realizing John's dream of the Benedictine Grange in West Redding, Connecticut. This book began with John's inspiration over twenty years ago, and I thank him for encouraging me to bring the seminal work forward to this fullness, made more beautiful by his evocative sketches.

It is an honor to have the words of my esteemed teacher, Father Thomas Berry, introduce this book of Merton's nature writings, since he is the prophet and poet of the new cosmology celebrated by Merton in these reflections. To him I owe my awakening to the glorious sacrality of this universe during my privileged time of study with him at Fordham University.

Special thanks to my insightful research partner, Ann Deignan, whose knowledge of Merton is rich and deep, and to her feline companion Galina who kept me company during the long days and nights given to the book. To Mary Anne Foley, CND, for her critical reading of my essay, and to Diana Breen and the staff of the Faculty Technology Resource Center at Iona College for their assistance, and to Dr. Michael Bard and Rick Pallidino, many thanks. Particular thanks are due to Anne McCormick, Secretary of the Merton Legacy Trust, for her guidance, to Brother Patrick Hart, OCSO, for his support, and to Jonathan Montaldo, Paul Pearson, and the encouraging colleagues and scholars of the International Thomas Merton Society. And of course to my wonderful editor Dan Driscoll and all the people at Sorin Books who have made this book a reality—a sincere thank you.

Finally a word of gratitude to my friends with whom I have enjoyed celebrating the mysteries of creation, from Skellig Micheal to Glendalough. Thanks to Don Bosco Mullan and Thomas O'Sullivan who brought me home to *Eire*; and to the *anam cara* who braved with me the wild Irish seas, and taught me the names of so many of the trees in Earth's garden.

Kathleen Deignan, CND, Ph.D.
Iona College, New Rochelle, NY
Lughnasadh, 2002

FOREWORD

Thomas Merton was twenty-six years old when, in 1941, he entered the first Cistercian Monastery founded in America. It was there in Kentucky that he began a writing career that extended from the mid-1940s until the mid-1960s. These were the years of existentialist angst in the thought world of Europe and North America, when such thinkers and writers as Jean-Paul Sartre, Albert Camus, Samuel Beckett, Arthur Miller, and Tennessee Williams in North America would deal with the darkest aspects in human life, when all illusions were removed. These were also the years of World War II, the Korean War, the Vietnam War, and the Cold War with the Soviet Union. Such was the larger context in which we must appreciate both Merton's life and the significance of his writings.

While he experienced his historical identity with all the various social and cultural movements of his times, he realized that his own unique calling did not permit him to be absorbed into any of the existing literary genres, nor with particular social controversies. Nor could he participate extensively with any of the more popular religious and spiritual movements that were swirling throughout these times.

His response was neither academic nor overly critical but spiritual in the most demanding sense of the word. While he did have extensive learning in the cultural and spiritual history of both the Western world and of Asia, he remained totally himself, writing mostly from the immediacy of his own experience. He knew that what was needed was a positive way out of these encompassing difficulties, much as Gandhi knew that a more spiritual way was needed to resolve the racial and social antagonisms of his times. The inner lucidity of his own insights, thoughts, and feelings was the secret of his impressiveness as a writer. This directness of style also enabled him to speak to the great variety of concerns that swept over the human community. He will always remain a unique personality, speaking a healing message to the variety of concerns of his own times and on into the future.

The volume of his writings in those twenty years indicate that he wrote immediately and coherently whenever time was available. The diversity of his writings indicates that he could think through a variety of issues from their most meaningful context. Perhaps the best way to think of Merton is in terms of a "post-critical naivete," the phrase suggested by the French philosopher Paul Ricoeur, who suggested this designation as a term that brings together the response of both innocence and experience as we pass through the unfolding events of these times.

He seems to have had some awareness of his early death, evidenced by the sense of urgency with which he wrote. His style is quiet and contemplative, but it moves rapidly, without hesitation through the sequence of his reflections. In presenting an overview of his writings in a symposium at Columbia University some years ago, I suggested that his writings might be presented under five categories.

First, in *The Seven Storey Mountain* he presented his own life as an archetypal pattern of conversion. Then in *The Waters of Siloe* he restored the mystical dimension of monastic spirituality—a monastic spirituality that had been tending, in the severity of its penitential discipline, toward excessive asceticism with almost a suspicion of any true mystical tradition.

Third, in *Conjectures of a Guilty Bystander* he presented his intimate presence to the social movements of his times. Fourth, in his poetry, but also in his drawings and his photography, he fostered an authentic Christian aesthetic that in his times had a tendency toward pietistic forms. His fifth achievement was to enable Christian and Asian spiritualities to be present to each other in a mutually supportive manner. This he accomplished in *Mystics and Zen Masters* and in *The Way of Chuang Tzu.*

In this overall view of Merton's writings I failed to include a category that would present his nature writings. To miss this aspect of his work was to fail in recognizing an all-pervasive aspect of his writings. Kathleen Deignan has now selected these writings as a distinctive category and given us a new way of appreciating Merton, not simply in some of his specific writings but in appreciating an all-pervasive concern throughout his work. This aspect of Merton takes on added significance since, in the future, the understanding of nature, its infinitely diverse modes of expression, and the need to develop a mutually enhancing mode of human presence to the natural world will be a central concern in every phase of human activity.

Kathleen Deignan provides a comprehensive reader that groups the various nature writings of Merton under their various subject matters. The variety of Merton's experiences covers almost the entire panorama of the natural world available in northern Kentucky, a wooded region somewhat near the shores of the Ohio River. That this western edge of the eastern woodlands beyond the Appalachian Plateau should be the setting in which Merton would experience the dawn and sunset, the chill of winter and the heat of summer, the fields and woodlands and the wilderness creatures, is itself significant. A little farther to the southwest begins the Great Central Valley, the greatest single feature of the North American continent, a valley that extends westward to the Rocky Mountains.

The monks who came to Kentucky in 1848 landed in New Orleans and traveled up the Mississippi River to the city of Louisville. They were from the French Abbey of Melleray, an abbey founded in the tradition of Saint Bernard of Clairvaux, one of the most outstanding religious leaders and also one of the most widely read authors of his time. Bernard, who died in 1153, and Hildegard of Bingen, who died in 1179, can be considered the two leading religious personalities of the twelfth century. Bernard was a dominant inspiration for Merton in both the nature and the style of his writing. Along with Hildegard, Bernard belongs among the medieval writers to whom the natural world is a central focus in his spiritual writings. The name of his monastery, Clairvaux—translated as "Clearview"—expresses his sensitivity in this regard.

Today, in the opening years of the twenty-first century, we find ourselves in a critical moment when the religious traditions need to awaken again to the natural world as the primary manifestation of the divine to human intelligence. The very nature and purpose of the human is to experience this intimate presence that comes to us through natural phenomena. Such is the purpose of having eyes and ears and feeling sensitivity, and all our other senses. We have no inner spiritual development without outer experience. Immediately, when we see or experience any natural phenomenon, when we see a flower, a butterfly, a tree, when we feel the evening breeze flow over us or wade in a stream of clear water, our natural response is immediate, intuitive, transforming, ecstatic. Everywhere we find ourselves invaded by the world of the sacred. Such was the experience of Thomas Merton. Such is the wonder that he is communicating to us.

An absence of a sense of the sacred is the basic flaw in many of our efforts at ecologically or environmentally adjusting our human presence to the natural world. It has been said, "We will not save what we do not love." It is also true that we will neither love nor save what we do not experience as sacred.

There is a certain futility in the efforts being made—truly sincere, dedicated, and intelligent efforts—to remedy our environmental devastation simply by activating renewable sources of energy and by reducing the deleterious impact of the industrial world. The difficulty is that the natural world is seen primarily for human use, not as a mode of sacred presence primarily to be communed with in wonder and beauty and intimacy. In our present attitude the natural world remains a commodity to be bought and sold, not a sacred reality to be venerated. The deep psychic change needed to withdraw us from the fascination of the industrial world, and the deceptive gifts that it gives us, is too difficult for simply the avoidance of its difficulties or the attractions of its benefits. Eventually only our sense of the sacred will save us.

Merton's gift, eloquently captured by Kathleen Deignan, is this sense of the sacred throughout the entire range of the natural world.

Thomas Berry
June 2002

"THE FOREST IS MY BRIDE"

The mystery of Thomas Merton's marriage to the forest is a rich and overlooked sub-theme in one of the most celebrated spiritual stories of modern times. A contemplative master of monumental fame and significance, Thomas Merton's life reads like a great drama in which all the crises and challenges of modernity are portrayed in the searching of one soul for liberation and wisdom. His 1948 autobiography *The Seven Storey Mountain*—resonating like the confessions of a modern American Augustine— introduced Merton to generations of readers around the world as the archetypal lost soul in search of union with God. His numerous personal journals and volumes of correspondence up to 1968 complete the masterful self-revelation of one man laboring for transformation and fullness of life in the confusions of the post-modern world.

The pathways he explored in his quest "to recover paradise" have become routes of discovery and healing for millions of seekers, and his prophetic voice on the perennial issues of violence, racism, commodity culture, ignorance, and psychic disorientation has pronounced saving wisdom that has changed the discourse and orientation of modern spirituality. All the turns in contemporary religious life toward mystical experience, engagement with the world in its woundedness and wonder, and the exchange of wisdom among the world's contemplative traditions were pioneered by Thomas Merton. He leaves a legacy of inspiring and challenging reports of daring explorations into farther reaches of the personal world, the social world, and the divine world. Curiously, what remains hidden or obscure in his very public discourse on matters of the sacred is the significance that the natural world played as the ecstatic ground of his own experience of God. But a close reading of his voluminous writings reveals his intimate rapport with and progressive espousal of creation as the body of divinity—at once veiling and unveiling the God he so longed to behold and be held by.

> . . . I live in the woods out of necessity. I get out
> of bed in the middle of the night because it is

imperative that I hear the silence of the night, alone, and, with my face on the floor, say psalms, alone, in the silence of the night.

. . . the silence of the forest is my bride and the sweet dark warmth of the whole world is my love and out of the heart of that dark warmth comes the secret that is heard only in silence, but it is the root of all the secrets that are whispered by all the lovers in their beds all over the world *(DWL,* p. 240).

Thomas Merton spent his whole monastic life listening for that secret pulsating in the heartbeat of creation, and wedded the forest so he could listen with absolute rapture and commitment as one would to a spouse, "for better, for worse, in sickness and in health, until death. . . ." What he heard in the murmurings of wilderness were "the sweet songs of living things" whose choirs he joined as a solitary monk offering a psalm of glory and thanksgiving on behalf of humankind. In time his own center became "the teeming heart of natural families" as his unique subjectivity opened to the cosmos in wonder and awe, sounding a silent interval of praise in the rapturous hymn of creation.

Thomas Merton's restless and passionate search for God took him through the traditions of monastic and hermitic life, intense engagements with the bloody struggles of the human enterprise, and the rich libraries of spiritual and cultural wisdom. Yet he found at last "the wide open secret" he yearned to know in the "present festival" of the natural world, in a wisdom that awakened in him an intimate "primordial familiarity" with creatures. He wrote no book explicitly to trace his route through creation to communion with divinity. Nor has any book been written about his journey. But one can identify certain influences that brought Merton to insist that the human vocation was ultimately to be "a gardener of paradise."

LANDSCAPE PAINTERS' SON

On the last evening of January 1915, with the stars in the sign of Aquarius, Thomas Merton was born during a snowstorm at the foot of a mountain in the Eastern Pyrenees. Mt. Canigou cast its shadow at the bottom of his garden, in a town called Prades in the Catalan lands of southern France near the border of Spain. His father was a New Zealander named Owen Merton and his mother, an American named Ruth Jenkins. Both were of Welsh ancestry and both were landscape painters. After the early death of his mother, Tom became his father's companion on many landscape-painting adventures, and as they toured the monastic ruins in the valleys of southern France he conceived his lifelong desire of attending to the great silence he experienced there. In fact, his father was his first and perhaps most influential teacher of contemplation, introducing Merton to the celebration of the sacred mysteries embodied in nature:

> His vision of the world was sane, full of balance, full of veneration for structure . . . and for all the circumstances that impress an individual identity on each created thing. His vision was religious and clean . . . since a religious man respects the power of God's creation to bear witness for itself (*SSM*, p. 11).

They traveled to the Mediterranean and down to the border of Catalonia, and then across an ocean to the tropics of Bermuda, and all the while young Tom was being tutored in the art of beholding. His father's mentorship influenced his abidingly vivid sense of geography and the confluence of art and nature in his sensibility. He inherited his father's intense and disciplined way of looking at the world, which Merton would later translate into a painterliness of language in describing it. Such training in "natural contemplation" became the foundation of his psychic life, and the ground of his experience of the divine, such that at an early age his religious instinct went skyward.

Day after day the sun shone on the blue waters
of the sea, and on the islands of the bay. I remember one day looking up at the sky, taking it into
my head to worship one of the clouds (*SSM*, pp.
30-31).

FRANCISCAN SOUL

Thomas Merton had a Franciscan soul, and this
realization grew in him over time. In the Christian
experience, Francis of Assisi personifies a way of celebrating familial intimacy with all the creatures of the
universe: Brother Sun, Sister Moon, Mother Earth.
Merton had his encounter with the Franciscan tradition in its intellectual form while an undergraduate
student at Columbia University in the 1930s, and it
inspired him to embrace Catholicism, and even more
dramatically to become a Franciscan. Under the mentorship of Dan Walsh he was introduced to the great
Franciscan intellectuals Bonaventure and Duns
Scotus, with whom Merton explicitly identified. Both
thinkers gave him necessary frameworks for understanding the hidden wholeness of creation, and
Bonaventure in particular presented to him an itiner-
ary for venturing in *The Soul's Journey into God*,
through the mysteries of creation, the self, and the
dark and trackless path of being. According to
Bonaventure, the sacred journey into God begins by

following the divine footprints back to their source as we "place our first step in the ascent on the bottom, presenting to ourselves the whole material world as a mirror through which we may pass over into God, the supreme Craftsman" (*SJG*, I, 9).

Merton moved in a similar sensibility, celebrating creatures as vestiges or sacraments that reflected the overflowing creativity of their divine Source. This is especially evident in *Seeds of Contemplation* where Merton describes creation as "the art of the Father." Likewise, his indebtedness to the Franciscan tradition is apparent in his poetry.

> For, like a grain of fire
> smoldering in the heart
> of every living essence
> God plants His undivided power—
> Buries His thought too vast
> for worlds
> In seeds and roots and blade
> and flower.
>
> —"The Sowing of Meanings,"
> *Figures for an Apocalypse*

In true Franciscan spirit, Merton could sense the "angelic transparency of everything, of pure, simple and total light." Son of the landscape artist that he was, Merton's aesthetic nature had a *kataphatic* orientation, delighting in the forms and images of the divine emanations. "We do not see the Blinding One in black emptiness," he writes in "Hagia Sophia," "He speaks to us gently in ten thousand things, the which His light is one fullness and one wisdom. Thus He shines not on them but from within them." Merton was intuitively drawn to this language of "inscape" discovered in the writing of Jesuit poet Gerard Manley Hopkins, who was himself temperamentally Franciscan and likewise greatly influenced by Duns Scotus. Merton echoes Hopkins' style in saying of creatures, "their inscape is their sanctity," and he sensed in all visible things "an invisible fecundity, a dimmed light, a meek namelessness, a hidden wholeness."

But nature also comforted and companioned Merton in his troubling orphanhood, as he discovered in the community of creatures a kinship circle he could be at home with. Only in the solitude of nature did Merton truly experience the peace and joy of his Franciscan soul. Only the simplicity of creation—that world of "sanity and perfection"— offered relief from his gnawing sense of alienation and burdensome habit of introspection. It provided for him a realm of freedom where he could be buoyant, light-hearted, and happy. The *kataphatic* way of glorious forms invited Merton to celebrate the liturgy of creation as joyful communicant, feasting on a kind of beauty and silence he tasted no other way, conducting him into divinity indwelling in all things. Nature evoked the poet and psalmist in him, and perhaps for these reasons Merton did not in fact ever join the Franciscans, but found his way to the woodland choir of a Cistercian monastery where the order of the day was simply to praise.

CISTERCIAN HEART

Thomas Merton entered the Trappist monastery of Our Lady of Gethsemani on December 10, 1941. An American foundation of the Cistercian order dedicated to the contemplative life, the monastery lands were set in the Appalachian region of Kentucky more remarkable for knobby woodlands than bluegrass. Merton came to this forest monastery to engage in a lifelong experiment in spiritual transformation by taking vows to harness and orient his energies of intention. Obedience, the primary Benedictine vow, directed the monk to listen with the ear of his heart to the still, small voice of God speaking in all things. Stability of place grounded the monk in a community of guidance that provided the holding environment for the great work. The more dynamic vow, *conversio morum*, set him to the daily labor of radical conversion to recover the authenticity of his true nature. To deepen these, the Cistercian monk entered into deep silence, which was for Merton a paradoxical opportunity for profound dialogue with the world and creation. Merton's promise of silence became a vow of conversation expressed in extraordinary literary creativity. During the twenty-seven years of his life at Gethsemani he became the most prolific monastic writer of all time. Understandably he sought refuge from the exhaustion of his own verbal intensity in the "wonderful, unintelligible, perfectly innocent speech" of nature that spoke its healing to him. It was creation's *lingua incognita* that relieved his ambivalence and compulsion toward human language and communication, at once intensifying and slaking his Cistercian thirst for the waters of silence described in his early history of the order:

> When the monks had found their homes, they not only settled there, for better or for worse, but they sank their roots into the ground and fell in love with their woods. . . . Forest and field, sun and wind and sky, earth and water, all speak the same silent language, reminding the monk that he is here to develop like the things that grow all around him . . . (*WS,* pp. 273-274).

Monasticism, east and west, was born in the woods and deserts of the earth. In so many of Merton's works he explores the impulse to the margins of inner and outer space that is a signature of the monastic temperament. In *The Wisdom of the Desert* he traces the roots of Christian monasticism to the deserts of the Middle East; in his essay "From Pilgrimage to Crusade" he tells of daring exploits of Celtic monks in search of their *dysarts* on the wild, remote islands of the North Atlantic. Merton shared this orientation toward the solitary places of divine encounter, and although Gethsemani was the lure that drew him toward it, eventually the conventional monastic enclosure frustrated more than satisfied his hunger for solitude and silence. But in 1951 in response to Merton's request for greater solitude, Abbot Dom James nominated him "forester" which entailed restoring the woodlands that had been stripped a decade earlier. The job radicalized his experience of solitude, no longer perceived as privacy for intellectual pursuits, but an opportunity for embodied engagement with a whole community of wisdom in silent participation in the vitality of living things. This charge, along with his reading of Thoreau, reawakened his desire to become a competent naturalist, which enhanced his other monastic commitments as husband of nature— planting, sowing, reaping, clearing, saving—and mentor of novices. In time he learned that the true mentor and spiritual director of souls was nature itself. The fields, rain, sun, sky, mud, clay, wind, and fire are all masters of sacred wisdom, and worthy subjects of contemplation.

Merton's espousal of the forest intensified in 1960 when he began to take up residence in a hermitage set on a knob called Mount Olivet. There his Cistercian heart found a wider community inviting him to the daily office of praise. Now his choir mates were frogs, birds, and cicadas—the "huge chorus of living beings (that) rises up out of the world beneath my feet: life singing in the watercourses, throbbing in the creeks and the fields and the trees, choirs of millions and millions of jumping and flying and creeping things" (*SJ*, p. 360). His worship became "a blue sky and ten thousand crickets in the deep wet hay of the field"; his vow became "the silence under their song" (*CA*, p. 6). Soon the whole landscape became the primordial scripture on which he meditated as he saturated "the country beyond words" with his psalms.

CELTIC SPIRIT

During the 1960s Merton began to sense what "writes the books, and drives me into the woods," and celebrated gratefully the Celtic spirit that coursed through his Welsh blood. In his discovery of Celtic monasticism he recognized himself in the hermits, lyric poets, and pilgrims of a tradition that opened a new world to him. He shared a similar spiritual temperament with these masters of "natural contemplation" (*theoria physike*) who sought God less in the ideal essences of things than in the physical hierophanic cosmos.

Though ever a romantic, his engagement with nature as farmer and forester was also tactile, athletic, even sensuous; like his father, he loved to walk barefoot in the woods, feeling the fragrant pine needles of Gethsemani beneath him. With the green martyrs of the Celtic tradition, he always enjoyed a palpable sense of the presence of the Presence for whom he and they had sacrificed the world of human society. It encircled him in the great encompassing of creation, and imparted to him a peace unlike any other. But his embrace of "green martyrdom" was never bucolic: his wedding to the solitude of the forest allowed this orphan man to feel in earnest the raw and excruciating wound of loneliness that widened and deepened with the years. He chose to live alone in the forest as refuge for his own existential pain, but also to make reparation for the violation of earth and earth peoples. Here he became a poet, a protester, a prophet, a political prisoner, and an escaped prisoner. Ever in search of his "true self" beneath his distress and artifice, he came in time to realize it was none other than his "green self"—his original nature healed of inner agitation, congestion, drivenness, turmoil, and suffering by entrainment to the merciful rhythms of the elements, the seasons, the creatures, in the particular bioregion of Kentucky that he called home.

Merton also identified with the Celtic monks' restless quest to recover paradise as a lived experience of the native harmony and unity of all beings. Indeed his lyrical language betrays his Celtic spirit playing at the "thin places" between the physical and imagined realms, as he allowed himself to be taken to in-between dimensions of sheer transparency where being sensibly flows through the courseways of creation, where time alters, where space opens to the numinous. And like his Celtic monastic ancestors he made "a profound existential tribute to realities perceived in the very structure of the world and of man, and of their being." In lineage with them, he engaged in that "spiritual dialogue between man and creation in which spiritual and bodily realities interweave and interlace themselves like manuscript illuminations in the Book of Kells" ("From Pilgrimage to Crusade," *MZM*, p. 97).

ZEN MIND

If Irish monks affirmed his Celtic spirit in their mastery of *kataphatic* contemplation of the wonders of divinity in nature, Buddhist monks evoked his Zen mind and drew him onto the *apophatic* path of formless "emptiness" he had begun to walk with Therese of Lisieux, Meister Eckhart, Teresa of Avila, John of the Cross, Julian of Norwich, the Desert Fathers and Mothers, and other Christian masters. From his days at Columbia, Merton had always entertained an attraction to the spiritualities of the East, and in the 1950s he began a serious study of Chinese humanism and Zen Buddhism. Within a decade he had written several books on the wisdom of Asia: *The Way of Chuang Tzu, Zen and the Birds of Appetite*, and *Mystics and Zen Masters*. As with so many other of his fascinations, he followed this one to its climax: his own death in Bangkok, Thailand, during a pan-monastic conference of Christians and Buddhists. As the Celtic monks made their lives a pilgrimage to their place of resurrection, Merton embarked on his voyage to the East in 1968 with an uncanny awareness of the destiny and ultimacy of this long desired journey. *The Asian Journal* reveals not only his readiness for the profound encounters and experiences that awaited him there, but the clear and simple state of mind to which his Zen studies had brought him.

Merton found in the teachings of Buddhism a direct method for dismantling the false, afflictive self that was the source of all personal, social, and even ecological suffering. As he experimented with forms of meditation and perception proposed by the Zen tradition, his consciousness began to transform. A Zen-like quality arose in his later writing on many subjects, but noticeably in his reflections on nature. The platonic intuition cultivated by Western masters began to yield to a direct, existential apprehension of the immediacy of things induced by Asian mentors like Chuang Tzu and Lao Tzu. The romanticism of his early years distilled to a spareness of observation. There was less interpretation, less "self" bleeding through the lean and spare verse; less narrative, because the narrator was disappearing. The great storyteller of "Monk's Pond" had no story to tell anymore; he was simply attending to the "wild being" he shared with creation, sensing it a "strange awakening to find the sky inside you and beneath you and above you and all around you so that your spirit is one with the sky" (*SJ*, p. 340).

Merton had recovered the *Tao*, the way of nature, in all its immediacy and transformative power, by the practice of self-forgetful attentiveness to creation that drew him out of his distorting mental preoccupations. This entrainment to nature brought him to his senses, letting him experience the naked vitality of life encompassing him on all sides. The incarnate word of each particular thing—with its own "suchness"—presented itself to him as a vibrant koan with which he wrestled in a gentle, playful way. In the process his perception was washed clean of mental and emotional formations that blurred his vision of the way things really are: impermanent, empty, self-less, undying.

The awakening of his Zen mind disclosed the deeper mystery of the God beyond concepts and images, intimated through a discipline of abandoning every name, every form, every concept of the divine. The fruit of this labor was a perception of the startling immediacy of an ever-incarnating divinity at once revealed and concealed in creation as mercy and love. He summarized the climax of his Asian journey—indeed, of his earthly pilgrimage—in a few spare words inscribed in his journal after his barefoot visit to the monumental Buddhas composed into the rocks and landscape of a garden in Polonnaruwa a few days before his death. In them he harvests the fruit of his Zen practice in his forest hermitage: "all problems are resolved and everything is clear, simply because what matters is clear. The rock, all matter, all life is charged with *dharmakaya* . . . everything is emptiness and everything is compassion."

THE RECOVERY OF PARADISE

Yearning for paradise was both a Celtic and Cistercian habit of heart that engaged Merton his whole life. Not an otherworldly quest, the recovery of paradise was realized in the awakening of a sense of communion in the mystery of life. He saw himself as a "New Adam" in the garden of the new creation, knowing and naming living things as his kin, saluting all species as the "innocent nations" that comprise the earth. Like a grateful celebrant, each morning at *"le point vierge"* (the virgin point) of dawn, he witnessed the rebirth of the cosmos "when creation in its innocence asks for permission to *be* once again." Thus awakened, wilderness was "another country" closer to Eden than any other he had ever known, where he "sat in stillness and loved the wind in the forest and listened for a good long while to God." There in the woods, he experienced himself at the center of the universe where at any

moment the gate of heaven would open wide and he would perceive the undying heavenliness in the real nature of things. "Paradise is all around," he heard the dawn deacon say: all we need do is enter in.

On each threshold of the encircling paradise awaited Sophia, "the Mother of all," the diffuse shining of God in creation. Merton understood her to be the personification of divinity at once hidden and manifest in all things. She was the eros that throbbed through countless creatures that mated, bore, and nurtured the infinity of cells in the body of God in their shape-shifting dynamics of praise. Her beauty and magnetism drew all beings into life as communion, as thanksgiving, as festival, as glory. As the very love that unifies the cosmos, Merton proclaimed Sophia "the Bride, the Feast, and the Wedding." It was she whom he espoused in her forest pavilion. In her embrace he experienced overpowering peace and delight, and the sweet dark warmth of the whole world became his great love. Thus he learned the secret of intimate communion "sent from the depths of the divine fecundity."

THOMAS MERTON'S
REFLECTIONS ON NATURE

If, as geologian Fr. Thomas Berry says, we have entered the "ecozoic age," it is important that global spirituality reflects and fosters a new sense of the sacrality of the natural world and of human identity within it. As in other issues of contemporary spiritu-ality, here too Merton leads the way. He wrote about his intimacy with creation in a style that is at once inspiring and instructive for other contemplatives in the world. In this his legacy is both accessible to and critical for modern people who labor toward a rebirth of our consciousness of and identity with creation, as an urgent spiritual and ecological necessity. Scattered throughout his journals, letters, and poetry are "seeds" of a vibrant creation spirituality in which Merton celebrates the natural world in all its variety, complexity, and beauty as the body of God. While this book does not present Merton's entire "nature corpus," it is intended to present the fruit of Merton's reflections on nature in the "seeds" of mystical insight gleaned in a contemplative reading of his personal reflections.

Thomas Berry has also reminded us that the original scripture is creation itself in its infinite unfolding of divine creativity. Each creature, as Merton notes, is a word of God. In these reflections he provides for us a gloss on the scripture of the cosmos, allowing nature to speak for itself, to speak to him and through him, as he engages with rapturous, disciplined attention, even and especially "when the trees say nothing." We are summoned likewise to attend the mysteries all around us and receive in the encounter all the peace and healing awaiting us there.

Perhaps Merton's writings on nature will awaken the naturalist in us, or the poet, or the creation mystic. Perhaps he will aid us in recovering our senses that were fashioned to behold the wonders all around us. Indeed these meditations will aid in healing the hurried, harried soul that has become divorced from the encompassing fullness in which divinity resides—at once concealed and revealed in the incarnate realm. In this as in those many other matters of the sacred, Merton is a spiritual master for us, offering a way to practice the art of natural contemplation by reading with delight and awe the scripture of creation unfolding moment by moment all about us. With him we enter into the liturgies of rain and autumn and dawn, discovering our own "thin places" where earth becomes diaphanous to Eden and finding there the sanity and refreshment that brings us true vitality.

In these reflections we hear not the voice of Merton the prophet rousing us to a new ecological responsibility, nor the voice of the guru delineating a clear route for contemplatives on the path of creation spirituality. Rather we hear the voice of the creation mystic inviting us to become part of the present festival, to join the general dance and embrace nature as the bride, the feast, and the wedding whom we espouse moment by moment in the healing art of attentiveness to her beauty and mystery.

CHAPTER 1

"TO KNOW LIVING THINGS"

1 In this wilderness I have learned how to sleep again. I am not alien. The trees I know, the night I know, the rain I know. I close my eyes and instantly sink into the whole rainy world of which I am a part, and the world goes on with me in it, for I am not alien to it.

2 How necessary it is for monks to work in the fields, in the rain, in the sun, in the mud, in the clay, in the wind: these are our spiritual directors and our novice-masters. They form our contemplation. They instill us with virtue. They make us as stable as the land we live in.

3 Another approach.

Yesterday I was sitting in the woodshed reading and a little Carolina wren suddenly hopped on to my shoulder and then on to the corner of the book I was reading and paused a second to take a look at me before flying away.

(Same wren just came back and is singing and investigating busily in the blocks of the wall over there.)

Here is what I think.

Man can know all about God's creation by examining its phenomena, by dissecting and experimenting and this is all good. But it is misleading, because with this kind of knowledge you *do not really* know the beings you know. You only know *about* them. That is to say you create for yourself a knowledge based on your observations. What you observe is really as much the product of your knowledge as its cause. You take the thing not as it is, but as you want to investigate it. Your investigation is valid, but artificial.

There is something you cannot know about a wren by cutting it up in a laboratory and which you can only know if it remains fully and completely a wren, itself, and hops on your shoulder if it feels like it.

A tame animal is already invested with a certain falsity by its tameness. By becoming what we want it to be, it takes a disguise which we have decided to impose upon it.

Even a wild animal, merely "observed," is not seen as it really is, but rather in the light of our investigation (color changed by fluorescent lighting).

But people who watch birds and animals are already wise in their way.

I want not only to observe but to *know* living things, and this implies a dimension of primordial familiarity which is simple and primitive and religious and poor.

This is the reality I need, the vestige of God in His creatures.

And the Light of God in my own soul.

And God in man's history and culture (but so mysteriously hidden there and so strangely involved in the Passion which He must suffer to redeem us from evil).

The wren either hops on your shoulder or doesn't. What he does—this he is. *Hoc est* [That it is].

And our ideas of Nature etc.? All very well, but *non est hoc, non est hoc* [it is not this, it is not this]. *Neti, Neti* [Neither this nor that].

Do no violence to things, to manipulate them with my ideas—to track them, to strip them, to pick something out of them my mind wants to nibble at. . . .

4 Our mentioning of the weather—our perfunctory observations on what kind of day it is, are perhaps not idle. Perhaps we have a deep and legitimate need to know in our entire being what the day is like, to *see it* and *feel it*, to know how the sky is grey, paler in the south, with patches of blue in the southwest, with snow on the ground, the thermometer at 18, and cold wind making your ears ache. I have a real need to know these things because I myself am part of the weather and part of the climate and part of the place, and a day in which I have not shared truly in all this is no day at all. It is certainly part of my life of prayer.

5 Two superb days. When was there ever such a morning as yesterday? Cold at first, the hermitage dark in the moonlight . . . a fire in the grate (and how beautifully firelight shines through the lattice-blocks and all through the house at night!). Then the sunrise, enormous yolk of energy spreading and spreading as if to take over the sky. After that the ceremonies of the birds feeding in the dewy grass, and the meadowlark feeding and singing. Then the quiet, totally silent day, warm mid morning under the climbing sun. It was hard to say psalms: one's attention was totally absorbed by the great arc of the sky and the trees and hills and grass and all things in them. How absolutely

true, and how central a truth, that we are purely and simply *part of nature*, though we are the part which recognizes God. It is not Christianity, indeed, but post-Cartesian technologism that separates man from the world and makes him a kind of little god in his own right, with his clear ideas; all by himself.

We have to be humbly and realistically what we are, and the denial of it results only in the madness and cruelties of Nazism, or of the people who are sick with junk and drugs. And one can be "part of nature" surely, without being Lady Chatterley's lover.

So that was one good day.

6 The other day there was a beautiful whistling of titmice—and now today one of them lay dead on the grass under the house, which may well have been some fault of mine, as we dumped some calcium chloride on a couple of anthills—not as a poison but as something to move them elsewhere. What a miserable bundle of foolish idiots we are! We kill everything around us even when we think we love and respect nature and life. This sudden power to deal death all around us *simply by the way we live*, and in total "innocence" and ignorance, is by far the most disturbing symptom of our time. I hope I at least can learn, but in the light of Holy Week I see, again, all my own internal contradictions—not all! Hardly! But the fact that I am full of them. And that we all are.

A phenomenal number of species of animals and birds have become extinct in the last fifty years—due of course to man's irruption into ecology.

There was still a covey of quail around here in early fall. Now I don't hear a single whistle, or hear a wing beat.

7 Bobbie A., a boy who came yesterday for two weeks—during his vacation—is about 15 with all the seriousness of 15: but serious about lizards, snakes, salamanders, birds, butterflies, all living, creeping, and flying things. We were out in the woods a little on my day of recollection and talking to him about these things was as good as praying.

8 Either you look at the universe as a very poor creation out of which no one can make anything or you look at your own life and your own part in the universe as infinitely rich, full of inexhaustible interest, opening out into infinite further possibilities for study and contemplation and interest and praise. Beyond all and in all is God.

Perhaps the book of life, in the end, is the book of what one has lived and if one has lived nothing, he is not in the book of life.

And I have always wanted to write about everything.

That does not mean to write a book that covers everything—which would be impossible. But a book in which everything can go. A book with a little of everything that creates itself out of everything. That has its own life. A faithful book. I no longer look at it as a "book."

9 In the silence of the countryside and the forest, in the cloistered solitude of my monastery, I have discovered the whole Western Hemisphere. Here I have been able, through the grace of God, to explore the New World.

10 The forms and individual characters of living and growing things, of inanimate beings, of animals and flowers and all nature, constitute their holiness in the sight of God.

Their inscape is their sanctity. It is the imprint of His wisdom and His reality in them.

The special clumsy beauty of this particular colt on this April day in this field under these clouds is a holiness consecrated to God by His own creative wisdom and it declares the glory of God.

The pale flowers of the dogwood outside this window are saints. The little yellow flowers that nobody notices on the edge of that road are saints looking up into the face of God.

This leaf has its own texture and its own pattern of veins and its own holy shape, and the bass and trout hiding in the deep pools of the river are canonized by their beauty and their strength.

The lakes hidden among the hills are saints, and the sea too is a saint who praises God without interruption in her majestic dance.

The great, gashed, half-naked mountain is another of God's saints. There is no other like him. He is alone in his own character; nothing else in the world ever did or ever will imitate God in quite the same way. That is his sanctity.

11 This morning I really opened the door of the *Duino Elegies* and walked in (previously I have only peeked in through the windows and read fragments here and there). For one thing I got the sound of the German really going, and got the feel of the First Elegy as a whole. . . . I think I needed this hill, this silence, this frost, to really understand this great poem, to live in it—as I have also in *Four Quartets*. These are the two modern poems, long poems, that really have a

great deal of meaning for me. . . . But the *Duino Elegies* and *Four Quartets* talk about my life itself, my own self, my own destiny, my Christianity, my vocation, my relation to the world of my time, my place in it. . . .

12 Again, sense of the importance, the urgency of seeing, fully aware, experiencing what is *here*: not what is given by men, by society, but is given by God and hidden by (even monastic) society. Clear realization that I must begin with these first elements. That it is absurd to inquire after my function in the world, or whether I have one, as long as I am not first of all alive and awake. And if that, and no more, is my job (for it is certainly every man's job), then I am grateful for it. The vanity of all false missions, when no one is sent. All the universal outcry of people who have not been told to cry out, but who are driven to this noise by their fear, their lack of what is right in front of their noses.

13 Obedient unto death. . . . Perhaps the most crucial aspect of Christian obedience to God today concerns the responsibility of the Christian, in a technological society, toward creation and God's creation and God's will for creation. Obedience to God's will for nature and for man—respect for nature

and love for man—in the awareness of our power to frustrate God's designs for nature and for man—to radically corrupt and destroy natural goods by misuse and blind exploitation, especially by criminal waste.

14 There is no question for me that my one job as a monk is to live this hermit life in simple and direct contact with nature, primitively, quietly, doing some writing, maintaining such contacts as are willed by God and bearing witness to the value and goodness of simple things and ways, loving God in all of it. I am more convinced of this than of anything else in my life and I am sure it is what He asks of me. Yet I do not always respond with perfect simplicity.

15 How beautiful it was last evening, the Vigil, with a long interval after collation. Since it was a fast day, we weren't long in the refectory in the evening, got out early and the sun was higher than it usually is in that interval, and I saw the country in a light that we usually do not see. The low-slanting rays picked out the foliage of the trees and high-lighted a new wheatfield against the dark curtain of woods on the knobs that were in shadow. It was very beautiful. Deep peace. Sheep on the slopes behind the sheep barn. The new trellises in the novitiate garden

leaning and sagging. A cardinal singing suddenly in the walnut tree, and piles of fragrant logs all around the woodshed, waiting to be cut in bad weather.

I looked at all this in great tranquility, with my soul and spirit quiet. For me landscape seems to be important for contemplation . . . anyway, I have no scruples about loving it.

Didn't St. John of the Cross hide himself in a room up in a church tower where there was one small window through which he could look out at the country?

CHAPTER 2

SEASONS

AUTUMN

1 Today it was colder: everywhere I went the sun seemed to be shining on buildings near me, showing them up bright and cold against dark slate clouds that sailed fast, torn into long patches of deep blue sky, behind them.

Going up 114th Street East of Amsterdam—there is a slight slope up, towards where there are a couple of trees and the wall of the heights and the drop; beyond that nothing but sky and parades of slate and purple and pigeon colored clouds: bright pale on the limestone of the Nurses Home, and my shadow going alongside of me on it, I can see by my shadow my hair is blowing, and thinking of the sky up ahead dark and turbulent as a sea, and a tree with a rim of leaves left scattered along the top of its fan of branches, nods and bends all northward, against that sky, "publishing," I think (making up a line but no poem to go with it) the trees ". . . publish the stern intentions of the fall."

2 Brilliant, windy day—cold. It is fall. It is the kind of day in October Pop used to talk about. I thought about him as I came up through the hollow, with the sun on the bare persimmon trees, and a song in my mouth. All songs are, as it were, one's last. I have been grateful for life. . . .

Great clouds of seeds fly in the wind from the poplar tree.

3 Evening. A turning point in the weather. The heavy rain clouds, broke up a bit in the morning. There were patches of sun, a few short showers late in the afternoon. It is turning cold. I noticed that my woodchuck had buried himself completely, covering up the entrance to his hole, and had gone to sleep for the winter in his bed of leaves. I wish him a happy sleep! And today is very autumn-like—cold clouds flying, trees half bare, wet leaves lying around everywhere, the broad valley beautiful and lovely. The wonderful, mysterious, lonely sense of an autumn evening. It is not the autumn of Rilke's poems, something hard, solid, yet more mysterious.

4 Hot, stuffy October weather, tense weather.

Bluejays scream in the pines. A big flicker with a smart black bib was rooting around in the grass outside the window.

Machines in the valley.

Wars in the weather. The machines will make war, when the days are tense like this. (I hear one making war on the soybeans.)

We have an instrument flying to Venus, and as it goes past, for thirty seconds it will have a view of the clouds. This will be in December. Then it will go on out nowhere, it will be an eye nowhere.

5 Today I am in a quiet, cool spot, in the shade of cottonwoods, short green grass, the red mesa to the right, forest in front, big vast mesa (Mesa del Viejo) behind. A profusion of yellow: flowering shrubs; sweet smell of sage brush; the gentle contemplative song of crickets. A beautiful autumn!

6 It may well be that this big fat book begins with the snow. The sky was gray and heavy with it, it was a gray sky full of not clouds, but snow. You couldn't tell what kept it from falling. It was the color of pewter, a frozen mist, with a pale, lined patch, where you might expect the sun.

Now that the trees are bare, or almost all bare, with only a few still bearing leaves, for contrast, the landscape is more interesting. You see hidden roads: what used to appear thick forests, are curtains of straight trees with fields in between. You can see the solid structure of the hills, their rocky flanks, the hard talus. And, along the top of the ridge, through the bare trees comes light. The landscape is more like a drawing and less like a painting. Sometimes it is like an architect's plan for a landscape, and that is what is interesting about it. The leaves have fallen and the landscape has analyzed itself out and the essentials of its structure are bare and clear.

The air also was cold this morning, and the river was so still that I threw acorns in it, and broke the reflection of a hill in perfect concentric rings.

Along the bank of the river, as I walked, I scared up some wild ducks out of the bushes, under the overhanging bank, and they flew out with beating wings and a kind of whirring cry over the still water of the river, and wheeled so that they disappeared and flew away concealed from me by scrub and bushes along the bank.

7 Blazing bright days, cool nights, my face still hot from burn as we sat yesterday at top of the long new farm cornfield . . . hills glimmering with heat and

color. Sky deep blue. All distances sharp. White dead corn leaves blowing about in the hot dust of the field, fully ravaged, fully harvested.

WINTER

1 Yesterday the first snow of the winter fell and last night before the Midnight Mass someone made me a furtive sign that it was snowing again. And so this morning is very beautiful, not because there is much snow, for it is as thin as sugar on the porridge of the monks under twenty-one who can't fast, and the grey grass comes through it everywhere. Nor is it beautiful because the sky is bright, for the sky is dark. But it is beautiful because of Christmas.

2 Now snow clouds are coming up in the west, and the bones of the hills in the south have snow on them and the trees are picked out sharply like iron bristles against a streak of pale, indifferent green sky. The alfalfa field in the bottoms is as green as watercress, streaked with snow. The evening is very silent.

3 Today, brilliant snow, never so blinding. Pale bright blue sky such as I have sometimes seen in England on rare days in East Anglia. All the trees are

heavy with snow and the hills hang like white clouds in the sky. But much of the snow has melted off the trees and there is a slight mist over the sunny valley. No jets, for a wonder, only a train off toward Lebanon. Quiet afternoon. Peace. May this Lent be blest with emptiness, peace and faith!

4 Looking out of the novitiate, when the winter sun is rising on the snowy pastures and on the pine woods of the Lake Knob, I am absorbed in the lovely blue and mauve shadows on the snow and the indescribably delicate color of the sunlit patches under the trees. All the life and color of the landscape is in the snow and sky, as if the soul of winter had appeared and animated our world this morning. The green of the pines is dull, verging on brown. Dead leaves still cling to the oaks and they also are dull brown. The cold sky is very blue. The air is dry and frozen. Instead of the mild, ambivalent winter of Kentucky, I breathe again the rugged cold of upstate New York.

5 The morning was dark, with a harder bluer darkness than yesterday. The hills stood out stark and

black, the pines were black over thin pale sheets of snow. A more interesting and tougher murkiness. Snowflakes began to blow when I went down to the monastery from the hermitage, but by 10:30 the sun was fairly out and it was rapidly getting colder.

By afternoon it looked like a New Year—with fresh, cold light and a biting wind burnishing the frozen snow.

6 The year struggles with its own blackness.

Dark, wet mush of snow under frozen rain for two days. Everything is curtained in purple greyness and ice. Fog gets in the throat. A desolation of wetness and waste, turning to mud.

Only New Year's Day was bright. Very cold. Everything hard and sparkling, trees heavy with snow. I went for a walk up the side of Vineyard Knob, on the road to the fire tower, in secret hope of "raising the sparks" (as the Hassidim say) and they rose a little. It was quiet, but too bright, as if this celebration belonged not to the new year or to any year.

More germane to this new year is darkness, wetness, ice and cold, the scent of illness.

But maybe that is good. Who can tell?

7 Days of gloomy and sunless cold. In the dusk of evening, walking out on the edge of my hill, with all

the hard outlines of this world lost in white snow, it
is like walking in space. Woods hang like clouds over
the invisible fields and bottoms.

8 Bleak leap-year extra day. Black, with a few
snowflakes, like yesterday (Ash Wednesday) when no
snow stayed on the ground but there was sleet and
the rain-buckets nearly filled. All the grass is white
with, not snow, death. . . .

Snowflakes meet on the pages of the Breviary.

9 The year of the dragon came in with sleet
crackling on all the quiet windows. The year of the
hare went out yesterday with our red fish kite twisting
and flapping in the wind over the Zen garden.

10 Cold grey afternoon, much snow, woods
bright with snow loom out of the dark, totally new
vision of the Vineyard Knob. Dark, etched out with
snow, standing in obscurity and in a kind of
spaciousness I had never seen before. The wide sweep
of snow on St. Benedict's field. I furiously climbed the
Lake Knob, wonderful woods! Slid down, tore my
pants on barbed wire, came back through the vast
fields of snow.

Sense of God all day.

11 The snow has stopped again. The full moon has risen in the blue, cold, evening sky. The snow all day, coming and going, falling and melting, has been March snow with dark scudding clouds and moments of brightness, and biting wind, and all the trees bending, and a fire in the fireplace.

12 After the rain, yesterday, the Presentation . . . it got cold and bright. Very cold in fact. It must have been about twenty when I went up to the hermitage to sleep—and apparently it was down around five or ten this morning. And now though the sun has been up for hours the grass still shines with thick frost. I observed the whiskers of frost on the dead cornstalks and on the creosoted gateposts. I walked out to the little pond in the ravine that goes through the knobs to [Herman] Hanekamp's old place, and walked about praying psalms on the dry salty place on the rise, where small pines are coming back in. Wasted, perhaps, time and film photographing an old root with inexhaustibly interesting forms, constructions and textures, in the weak sun.

13 Whorled dark profile of a river in snow. A cliff in the fog. And now a dark road straight through a long fresh snow field. Snaggy reaches of snow

pattern. Claws of mountain and valley. Light shadow or breaking cloud on snow. Swing and reach of long, gaunt, black, white forks.

14 The first Sunday of Lent, as I now know, is a great feast. Christ has sanctified the desert and in the desert I discovered it. The woods have all become young in the discipline of spring: but it is the discipline of expectancy only. Which one cut more keenly? The February sunlight, or the air? There are no buds. Buds are not guessed at or thought of, this early in Lent. But the wilderness shines with promise. The land is dressed in simplicity and strength. Everything foretells the coming of the holy spring. I had never before spoken so freely or so intimately with woods, hills, birds, water, and sky. On this great day, however, they understood their position and they remained mute in the presence of the Beloved. Only His light was obvious and eloquent. My brother and sister, the light and water. The stump and the stone. The tables of rock. The blue, naked sky. Tractor tracks, a little waterfall. And Mediterranean solitude. I thought of Italy after my Beloved had spoken and was gone.

SPRING

1 Heavy snowflakes fall, flying in all directions. But when there is no wind they descend so slowly that they seem determined not to land on the ground. When in fact they do touch the ground they vanish completely. Then the pale sun comes out for a moment, shines uncertainly on the grass, the wheel, the pale pine logs, the rusty field, the fence, the valley. It is St. Benedict's, the first day of spring.

2 Real Spring weather—these are the precise days when everything changes. All the trees are fast beginning to be in leaf and the first green freshness of a new summer is all over the hills. Irreplaceable purity of these few days chosen by God as His sign!

3 Today was *the* prophetic day, the first of the real shining spring: not that there was not warm weather last week, not that there will not be cold weather again. But this was the day of the year when spring became truly credible. Freezing night, but cold bright morning, and a brave, bright shining of sun that is new, and an awakening in all the land, as if the earth were aware of its capacities!

I saw that the woodchuck had opened up his den and had come out, after three months or so of sleep, and at that early hour when it was still freezing. I thought he had gone crazy. But the day proved him right and me wrong.

The morning got more and more brilliant and I could feel the brilliancy of it getting into my own blood. Living so close to the cold, you feel the spring. And this is man's mission! The earth cannot feel all this. We must. But living away from the earth and the trees we fail them. We are absent from the wedding feast.

4 It is gray and cold again, but there have been warm spring days and spring is now irreversible. The crocuses are bunched together in the cold wet grass. I saw my Towhee in the bushes the other day— silent—but today I heard him, and his discreet, questioning chirp, in the rose hedge. There is a solitary mocking bird, apparently with no mate, that patrols the whole length of the rose hedge and tries to keep every other bird from resting there.

5 A lovely spring morning. Things really getting to be green, just before they fully clothe themselves in foliage. I see a little stand of timid willows picked out thinly in the sun along the creek in the bottoms, against the shadow of the opposite hill.

6 Easter Day, grey and stuffy; ended in thunderstorms while I was having supper (and reading the *Confessions of Zeno*). Yesterday was cool and clear, and today too, the same bright, sharp, cool dawn full of birdsong. Every thing is breaking into leaf, the dogwoods are coming out, the flowers still greenish white (the one in the monastery yard is the first one to be fully white). Yesterday I went for a walk over to the distant little hidden pond on Linton's farm and stood there a while in the sun.

7 A beautiful spring day—one of those than which no more beautiful is possible. Everything green and cool (a light frost in the early morning). Bright sun, clear sky, almost everything now fully in leaf except that some of the oaks are still silver rather than green.

8 When warmth comes again to the sea the Tritons of spring shall wake. Life shall wake underground and under sea. The fields will laugh, the woods will be drunk with flowers of rebellion, the night will make every fool sing in his sleep, and the morning will make him stand up in the sun and cover himself with water and with light.

9 We are now in the most perfect days of the Appalachian spring, late April: days of dogwood and redbud blossoms. Cool clear days with every delicate shade of green and red in the thinly budding branches of the oaks and maples. Later, in the burnt haze of summer, Kentucky's soaked green will be monotonous as a jungle, turning brown in the heat. Now it is France, or England. The hills suddenly look like the Cotswolds.

10 What a beautiful Spring it has been. A late cold spring, sometimes rainier than usual. Sunday morning after Mass, sitting in the quiet novitiate chapel, with the sun coming in through the East windows and a warm dark rain blowing up against the West windows and embracing the whole building in a great rumor.

The lovely leaves of the young linden we planted two years ago, fresh green against the dark hills, yesterday, when it was cloudy.

The new shrine of St. Fiacre, and the laburnum we planted near it. The laburnum already begins to be full of promise.

The maple we planted down the hill, beginning to flourish in virginal splendor. And all the other young trees that God planted down there, stretching out their arms with joy—and the small leaves coming out all over them.

The great wind that blew on the building all the other night, rattling the doors in the darkness. The goldfinch that flew across the garden. The titmouse in the woodshed with a short ebony beak, and very soft grey plumage and the inexpressible rose tint about the belly, if a titmouse has a belly. It came within three feet of my foot as I sat on the saw-rig. Very friendly, or rather, that is wrong: the wonderful unpredictable curiosity of birds which we desecrate by reading into it motives from our own psychology.

11 After four or five grim wet days, cold and dark, suddenly bright spring—cold, clear blue sky with a few very clean, well-washed clouds. Thin and full of light. The wet earth is springy, green moss shows in the short grass under the pines. The frogs sang for a moment (but it is still cold). The buds are beginning to swell. A flycatcher was playing in the woods near the stile as I came up, and the pileated woodpecker, bright combed, darted out, swinging up and down over the field to the east.

12 Warm—first thundershowers of the year, after low clouds moved fast and evenly all across the sky. Now rain chasing itself across the valley like smoke. And a quiet, peaceful roaring in the woods. Rain drops busily in the buckets. Yesterday, the first

Sunday of Lent, was a real spring day, the first. Warm sun, and a chipmunk sitting on a rock in the woods.

13 Today has the sort of clean sky and coldness of air and brightness all over, to make all things sharp and every line keen shapes firm colors bright that fall has. The effect was funny on me; I have been playing spring and so has the weather. . . .

SUMMER

1 Wind and sun. Catbird bickering in a bush. Ringing bells and blowing whistles and then squawking in a lamentable fashion. Trees are all clothed and benches are out and a new summer has begun.

2 A sweet summer afternoon. Cool breezes and a clear sky.

This day will not come again.

The young bulls lie under a tree in the corner of their field.

Quiet afternoon. Blue hills. Day lilies nod in the wind.

This day will not come again.

3 How high the corn is this year, and what joy there is in seeing it! The tall crests nodding twelve to fifteen feet above the ground, and all the silk-bearded ears. You come down out of the novitiate, through the door in the wall, over the trestle and down into this green paradise of tall stalks and silence. I know the joy and the worship the Indians must have felt, and the Eucharistic rightness of it! How can one *not* feel such things—so that I love the Mayas and Incas as perhaps the most human of peoples, as the ones who did most honor to our continents.

The irreligious mind is simply the *unreal* mind, the zombie, abstracted mind, that does not see the things that grow in the earth and feel glad about them, but only knows prices and figures and statistics. In a world of numbers you can be irreligious, unless the numbers themselves are incarnate in astronomy and music. But for that, they must have something to do with seasons and with harvests, with the joy of the Neolithic peoples who for millennia were quiet and human.

Great cumulus clouds piled up over the valley, high as Mont Blanc, and probably as cool. Looked at them while thinking over my reading from Banya Ibn Peguda—Spanish 11th century Jew, who wrote in Arabic.

4 Coming home—through Shakertown, Harrodsburg, Perryville and Lebanon. Beautiful June countryside—deep grass and hay, flowering weeds, tall cumulus clouds, corn a foot high and beautifully green tobacco struggling to begin. The old road between Perryville and Lebanon—winding between small farms and old barns, with wooded knobs nearby, is one I like. After Lebanon, thundershowers,

heavy rain and black sky over the fields to the north, with much lightning. Country people in the streets of Lebanon (Saturday afternoon). It was a nice ride. Coming through Pleasant Hill without stopping, saw new aspects of the wonderful Shaker houses—inexhaustible variety and dignity in sameness.

5 Hot. Yesterday, the dip in the path to the woods beyond the sheep barn was like an oven. The breeze like the breath of a furnace.

6 Another August has ended and we will never see it again. It was hot and stuffy all day, but although it did not rain, after Vespers the air was cooler and the sky had brushed up to look something like September. O frightening and beautiful month with Saint Giles standing in your door to be the patron of those who are afraid. Soon we will fight the fields of corn.

CHAPTER 3

ELEMENTS

EARTH

1 O Earth! O Earth! When will we hear you sing,
Arising from our grassy hills?
And say: "The dark is gone, and Day
Laughs like a bridegroom in His tent, the lovely sun!
His tent the sun! His tent the smiling sky!"

How long we wait, with minds as dim as ponds,
While stars swim slowly homeward in the waters
        of our west?
O Earth! When will we hear you sing?

How long we listened to your silence in our
        vineyards,
And heard no bird stir in the rising barley.
The stars go home behind the shaggy trees:
Our minds are grey as rivers.

O Earth, when will you wake in the green wheat,
And all our oaks and Trappist cedars sing:
"Bright land! Lift up your leafy gates!
You Abbey steeple, sing with bells,
For look, our Sun rejoices like a dancer
On the rim of our hills!"

In the blue west, the moon is uttered like the word
"Farewell."

2 The hills are suddenly dark blue. Very green alfalfa in the bottoms. Yellow or mustard or siena sage grass in my own field. Here there is no impatience. I am a submerged dragon. The peace of the Alleluias.

3 On Sunday I took one of the two torn raincoats that hang in the grand parlor for the use of the monks, and went out into the woods. Although I had not at first determined to do so, I found myself climbing the steepest of the knobs, which also turned out to be the highest—the pyramid that stands behind the head of the lake, and is second in line when you begin to count from the southwest. Bare woods and driving rain. There was a strong wind. When I reached the top I found there was something terrible about the landscape. But it was marvelous. The completely unfamiliar aspect of the forest beyond our rampart

unnerved me. It was as though I were in another country. I saw the steep, savage hills, covered with black woods and half buried in the storm that was coming at me from the southwest. And ridges traveled away from this center in unexpected directions. I said, "Now you are indeed alone. Be prepared to fight the devil." But it was not the time of combat. I started down the hill again feeling that perhaps after all I had climbed it uselessly.

Halfway down, and in a place of comparative shelter, just before the pine trees begin, I found a bower God had prepared for me like Jonas's ivy. It had been designed especially for this moment. There was a tree stump, in an even place. It was dry and a small cedar arched over it, like a green tent, forming an alcove. There I sat in silence and loved the wind in the forest and listened for a good while to God.

4 I came home walking along the shelves of shale that form the bed of the creek. Our woods are beautiful. The peace of the woods almost always steals over me when I am at prayer in the monastery.

5 All the hills and woods are red and brown and copper, and the sky is clear, with one or two very small clouds. A buzzard comes by and investigates me, but I am not dead yet. This whole landscape of

woods and hills is getting to be saturated with my prayers and with the Psalms and with the books I read out here under the trees, looking over the wall, not at the world but at our forest, our solitude.

6 On the flight from Dallas—Northern Texas and Arkansas—(Red River, Arkansas River)—there were floods everywhere, calligraphies of birds and oxbows and lakes and flooded fields. Later—the lovely patterns of lighted towns. Everything greener and greener, and today, with all the grass knee deep and the young trees having grown a foot in two weeks, I scarcely recognized Kentucky. The Bardstown Road was almost unfamiliar, and I had a hard time adjusting to it. This evening—it is a wonder to see the cumulus clouds over the green hills in the south, and to live again in a forest of hard woods, of oaks, elms, maples and hickories.

7 Peace and beauty of Easter morning: sunrise, deep green grass, soft winds, the woods turning green on the hills across the valley (and here too). I got up and said the old office of Lauds, and there was a wood thrush singing fourth-tone mysteries in the deep ringing pine wood (the "unconscious" wood) behind the hermitage. (The "unconscious" wood has a long moment of perfect clarity at dawn, and from

being dark and confused, lit from the east it is all clarity, all distinct, seen to be a place of silence and peace with its own order in disorder—the fallen trees don't matter, they are all part of it!)

8 We flew South West over the big river, with our propellers ringing a halo of ice around the sinking sun. I challenged the country below to tell us something about my destiny. These were fiercer fields, all on hills. The slanting rays of the sun picked out the contours of the land, with waves and waves of hills flying away from the river, skirted with curly woods or half-shaved like the backs of poodles, farms sitting in the crooks of valleys or under the elbows of wooded elevations, and dirt roads twisting to them through the fields. Thus I knew that I was in my state again, which is Kentucky.

A I R

1 Evening: cold winter wind along the walls of the chapel. Not howling, not moaning, not dismal. Can there be anything mournful about wind? It is innocent, and without sorrow. It has no regrets. Wind is a strong child enjoying his play, amazed at his own strength, gentle, inexhaustible, and pure. He

burnishes the dry snow, throwing clouds of it against the building. The wind has no regrets. The chapel is very cold. Two die-hard novices remain there alone, kneeling both upright, very still, no longer even pretending to enjoy or to understand anything.

2 And now my whole being breathes the wind which blows through the belfry, and my hand is on the door through which I see the heavens. The door swings out upon a vast sea of darkness and of prayer. Will it come like this, the moment of my death? Will You open a door upon the great forest and set my feet upon a ladder under the moon, and take me out among the stars?

3 The year of the dragon has so far distinguished itself by strong, lusty winds—great windstorm the other night, some trees blew down in the woods near the hermitage (one across the path going up). Pine cones and bits of branches all over the lawn. And last night too, great strong winds fighting the side of the building. I still hear them grumbling around outside like friendly beasts. Moon at 3:30, over the cold garden full of wind.

4 The woods all smell of malt because the South wind blows, bringing us news of the distillery a mile

away. Clouds in the sky. It will rain and tomorrow will suddenly be cold and the year's end will be upon us. Already the leaves seem to be changing color—and they are, not because it is fall. They were dried up by the dry summer.

5 Hot dry wind, still no rain. There are supposed to be tornadoes in Indiana. Cloudy sky, sinister fallout-like mist, humidity, wind, and no rain. You can hardly see across the valley.

FIRE

1 Flames springing up in the leaves across the creek like the spread of attachments in an unmortified soul!

So, *confortetur cor tuum et viriliter age!* Here are the things that must be done:

Many lights are burning that ought to be put out.

Kindle no new fires. Live in the warmth of the sun.

2 White smoke rising up in the valley, against the light, slowly taking animal forms, with a dark background of wooded hills behind. Menacing and peaceful, probably brush fires, maybe a house, probably not

a house. Cold, quiet morning, watch ticks on the desk. Produce nothing.

3 Fire last Wednesday in the knobs behind our own hills. We went out, and climbed through the forest, and I and the novices never made it to the right knob, saw smoke snaking along it, went around by the road to get nearer and missed it. We were overtaken by dark in strange woods but did not get lost. Later: the hill that had been burned stood like a city huge in the dark and the still burning stumps were like lighted buildings.

4 The other day I was out there with an axe and there were big fires all down the side of the little hill where the wayside shrine is, and the secular cemetery. The flames were angry and high and one delicate sapling which was left standing in the midst of all the fires withered and was blasted in the burning air. I watched the shuddering of the leaves in the gusts of that furnace and it made me think of Saint Joan of Arc.

5 Then as it got dark I saw that the hills across the valley were at one place covered with a wide warm circle of biting and rapidly advancing red flame in a big sweep half a mile across or more. This morning the fire was there but the perimeter was broken and

there was a flame wandering jaggedly eastward. Before dawn even that was gone. Either men fought it all night, or else the dew got so heavy that everything was too wet.

6 This evening before Vespers low gray clouds, very dark, all the woods and bottoms looked grim, but there was a brushfire along the road that skirts the ridge of Mount Olivet, and you could see the jagged bloody wound of flames eating its way among the trees, with blue smoke pouring out over the road and the pasture. It was a strange and beautiful background for the Sorrowful Mysteries of the Rosary.

7 Yesterday—bright sun—I took seven scholastics out to burn cedar brush in the woods, allotted to us as our little portion. Today, after dinner, under a grey cold sky, I went out there and found the fire still smouldering under the fine silver-grey ash. I stirred up the ashes and sat by the fire with the wind blowing on my back and read about the humility of the Desert Fathers, and presently it began to snow. I had been praying to Our Lady for strength and perseverance.

8 The weather is warmer. Have made beautiful brushfires behind the sheep barn, with great tides of

flames swimming from side to side in the warm wind. Fires of cedar brush, where we cut down trees this Winter. Less luck in burning the old wet piles of oak branches left two Winters ago by Bro. Bruno behind the lake that leaks—massive, sodden piles of wood and wet mulch. The leaves on the top catch and the whole thing is briefly washed in fire, then the fire dies and nothing is left but blackness and smoke.

WATER

1 In front of St. Anne's a brook runs through the ashes of the fire where we burned cedar branches and the bones of a cow at the year's end. The bottoms are flooded. Now rivers decided to traverse in every direction, the plowed fields. A great white bird comes flying over these waters as if it had suddenly found its way here, with the rain clouds, from some distant sea.

2 Meadowlarks singing in the snow, along the road from the cowbarns. Cold water of the stream, full of sun, over green watercress between banks of snow. Blue water of the lake, very blue, and blinding with sun, along the edge of the sheet of melting ice, covered with snow.

3 Heavy and steady rain with high winds for two days on end, and much rain before that. The Ohio Valley is probably flooded. Here, there is water everywhere. Streams come from everywhere and all night the air is full of the rushing of water and of wind. Wonderful black skies hang over the woods and there is a great strong expectancy of spring in all the wet black trees. There is a yellow waterfall rushing over the new dam down at the waterworks.

4 Reincarnation or not, I am as tired of talking and writing as if I had done it for centuries. Now it is time to listen at length to this Asian ocean. Over there, Asia.

CHAPTER 4

FIRMAMENT

SKY AND CLOUDS

1 The evening sky over the valley. Long lines of clouds travelling in strong cold wind toward the east.

Janua Coeli [Gate of Heaven]. How different prayer is here. Clarity—direction—to Christ the Lord for the great gift—the passage out of this world to the Father, entry into the kingdom. I know what I am here for.

May I be faithful to this awareness. *"Le project initial?"* ["The initial project?"]

2 It is a strange awakening to find the sky inside you and beneath you and above you and all around you so that your spirit is one with the sky, and all is positive night.

Here is where love burns with an innocent flame, the clean desire for death: death without sweetness, without sickness, without commentary, without reference and without shame. Clean death by the sword of the spirit in which is intelligence. And everything in order. Emergence and deliverance.

3 There has been no sun in the sky since New Year's but the dark days have been magnificent. The sky has been covered with wonderful black clouds, the horizon has been curtained with sheets of traveling rain. The landscape has been splendidly serious. I love the strength of our woods, in this bleak weather. And it *is* bleak weather. Yet there is a warmth in it like the presence of God in aridity of spirit, when He comes closer to us than in consolation.

4 It was raining and there was a wind. I went out to the wagon shed. You could still see the hills in the distance, not too much rain for that—many black clouds, low and torn, like smoke from a disaster, flying angrily over the wide open ruin of the old horsebarn, where I now love to walk alone. On sunny days it does not have this Castle of Otranto look about it.

5 A wonderful sky all day, beginning with the abstract expressionist Jackson Pollock dawn. Scores of streaks and tiny blue-gray clouds flung like blotches all over it. Before my conference . . . deep clear blue sky with astonishing small luminous clouds, than which I never saw lighter and cleaner! Exhilarating coolness and airiness of these little clouds!

6 Before sunset I walked in the field and looked at the sea of bluish steam about 1000 feet deep that hangs over everything, with a few pink cloud-bergs standing up high out of it in the cleaner blue. This afternoon—signs of a storm but it went away with hardly a growl.

7 Clouds running across the face of the waning moon. Distant flashes of lightning. I know what it is: a "warm front," etc. Clouds running over the face of the waning moon. And who cares what the weather may be? It is money that cares about weather and pays to predict it, perhaps someday to control it. And who wants a world in which weather is controlled by money?

8 All week, warm days, like spring. Then today, rain all day. This evening the storm is breaking up. Long low blue-black clouds came trailing up over the black ridge out of Tennessee, low and fast, streaming to the North. I stood and watched them in my evening meditation. Perfect silence, but for a dog barking far down the valley somewhere, towards Newton's.

9 In the Night, a rumpled thin skin of cloud over the sky; not totally darkening the moon. It has become thicker as the morning wears on. There is a feeling of snow in the air. Streaks of pale, lurid light over the dark hills in the south. The SAC plane sailed low over the valley just after the bell for consecration at the conventual Mass and an hour later another one went over even nearer, almost over the monastery. Enormous, perfect, ominous, great swooping weight, grey, full of Hiroshimas and the "key to peace."

10 Troops of small lavender clouds in an obedient procession go off east before a warm wind. The night has been rainy but the morning star shines clear in the gaps of clouds and the troops are ending raggedly.

11 Day after day the sun shone on the blue waters of the sea, and on the islands of the bay, and on the white sand at the head of the bay, and on the little white houses strung along the hillside. I remember looking up into the sky, and taking it into my head to worship one of the clouds, which was shaped at one end like the head of Minerva with a helmet—like the head of the armed lady on the big British pennies.

12 For my part my name is that sky, those fence-posts, and those cedar trees. I shall not even reflect on who I am and shall not say my identity is nobody's business because that implies a truculence I don't intend. It has no meaning.

Now my whole life is this—to keep unencumbered. The wind owns the fields where I walk and I own nothing and am owned by nothing and I shall never even be forgotten because no one will ever discover me. This is to me a source of immense confidence.

13 Today, unless I am mistaken, is the feast of Blessed John Ruysbroeck—or would be if he had one. The morning sky behind the new horsebarn was as splendid as his writing. A thousand small high clouds went flying majestically like ice-floes, all

golden and crimson and saffron, with clean blue and aquamarine behind them, and shades of orange and red and mauve down by the surface of the land where the hills are just visible in a pearl haze and the ground was steel-white with frost—every blade of grass as stiff as wire.

14 This morning, under a cobalt blue sky, summer having abruptly ended, I am beginning the Book of Job. It is not warm enough to sit for long in the shade of the cedars. The woods are crisply outlined in the sun and the clamor of distant crows is sharp in the air that no longer sizzles with locusts.

15 North, toward Shelter Cove, a manufactory of clouds where the wind piles up smoky moisture along the steep flanks of the mountains. Their tops are completely hidden.

Back inland, in the Mattole Valley at the convent, it is probably raining. South, bare twin pyramids. And down at the shore, a point of rock on which there is a silent immobile convocation of seabirds, perhaps pelicans.

Far out at sea, a long low coastal vessel seems to get nowhere. It hangs in an isolated patch of light like something in eternity.

SUN AND MOON

1 The sun is rising. All the green trees are full of birds, and their song comes up out of the wet bowers of the orchard. Crows swear pleasantly in the distance, and in the depths of my soul sits God.

2 Sunrise: hidden by pines and cedars to the east: I saw the red flame of the kingly sun glaring through the black trees, not like dawn but like a forest fire. Then the sun became distinguished as a person and he shone silently and with solemn power through the branches, and the whole world was silent and calm.

3 The sun is rising in streaks of dirty mist. If I had never seen a Japanese print, I would probably have experienced this in a purely Western way. The sun as one thing among many, a multitude of trees, enclosure wall in the foreground. But Sumiye makes this whole view one. One—a unity seen because the sun is in the center, a unity which is more than the total of a number of parts.

4 The sun is bright. Catbirds sing with crazy versatility above my head in the tree. Fasting *is easy in nice weather.*

5 A tremendous, bright sky. I let the warm sun shine on my back. The hills were wonderful. All the green of green things is clean and dark and fresh and the sun is so high on the elliptic that the shadows of things are right under them. Under my feet is the richness of all the new crushed limestone, or whatever it is that has been put on all the paths in the garden.

6 Tonight the new moon was shining in the west; and really new.

Although men have seen the same moon for more than a million years. That is one of the good things about being in the woods, living by the sun, moon and stars, and gladly using the moonlight, which should now be available for some three weeks on clear nights at the beginning or at the end.

I am surprised how easy it is to follow a familiar path even by starlight alone.

7 Last night went down to the offices of the Easter Vigil by full moonlight and came back also by full moonlight, the woods being perfectly silent, and the moon so strong one could hardly see any stars. I sat

on the porch to make my thanksgiving, after communion.

8 There was an eclipse of the moon about 4 to 5 this morning. The clouds cleared a little and I was able to see it begin. Then after I said Mass I went out and the eclipse was closer to full, the clouds had almost completely gone. The moon was beautiful, dimly red, like a globe of almost transparent amber, with a shapeless foetus of darkness curled in the midst of it. It hung there between two tall pines, silent, unexplained, small, with a modest suggestion of bloodiness, an omen without fierceness and without comment, pure.

9 Clear, thin new moon appearing and disappearing blue clouds—and the living black skeletons of the trees against the evening sky. More artillery than usual whumping at Knox. It is my fifty-third birthday.

10 Last night, full moon. At midnight the whole valley was drenched in silence and dark clarity. Cold this morning. Going down to the monastery in the dark I could feel frost on the grass and the dry corn husks under my feet.

PLANETS AND STARS

1 Riches! The comet. I went out and though there was mist I saw it as it first began to appear. Later it became more definite and quite bright (what I am seeing is the reflection of the comet's tail for it is now past the sun). A most beautiful and moving thing this great spear in the sky pointing down to the horizon where the sun will not appear yet for an hour and a half. As I watched, under the oaks, with acorns dropping around me, the bell rang in church for the preface and consecration. Three meteorites flashed across the sky in fifteen minutes. Two army transports growled and blinked across the comet's path, and the stag cried out in the dark field beyond my hedge. Riches! I recited Psalm 18, *coeli enarrant* [let the heavens proclaim]—with joy.

2 Very cold morning, about 8 above zero. Left for the hermitage before dawn, after retreat conference on sin. Pure dark sky with only moon and planets in it, stars already gone. The moon and Venus over the barns, and Mars far over in the west over the road and the fire tower.

3 This is the kairos, say the stars, says Orion, says Aldebaran, says the sickle moon rising behind the dark tall cedar cross. And I remember the words I said to Father Philotheus, which may have been in part a cliché but they were very sincere and I knew at the time that I really meant them and they were unpremeditated. I said, "I want to give God everything." Until now, I really have not. Or perhaps, in a way, I have tried to, but certainly not hard enough.

4 Cooked supper at the hermitage. . . . In fact cooked too much rice, having miscalculated, and sat half an hour consuming it, with tea. But it was a splendid supper (looking out at the hill in the clear evening light). After that, washing dishes—the bowl, the pot, the cup, the knife, . . . the spoon—looked up and saw a jet like a small rapid jewel travelling north between the moon and the evening star—the moon being nearly full. Then I went for a little walk down to my gate (about 100 yards) and looked out over the valley. Incredibly beautiful and peaceful. Blue hills, blue sky, woods, empty fields, lights going on in the Abbey, to the right through a screen of trees, hidden from the hermitage.

5 Bright morning—freezing, but less cold than before—and with a hint of the smell of spring-earth in the cold air. A beautiful sunrise, the woods all peaceful and silent, the dried old fruits on the yellow poplar shining like precious artifacts. I have a new level in my (elementary) star-consciousness. I can now tell where constellations may be in the daytime when they are invisible. Not many, of course! But for example: the sun is rising in Aquarius and so I know that in the blue sky overhead the beautiful swan, invisible, spreads its wide wings over me. A lovely thought, for some reason.

6 It is turning into the most brilliant of winters.

At 6:45 stepped out into the zero cold for a breath of air. Dark. Brilliance of Venus hanging as it were on one of the dim horns of Scorpio. Frozen snow. Deep wide blue-brown tracks of the tractor that came to get my gas tank that other day when everything was mucky. Bright hermitage settled quietly under black pines.

7 Zero yesterday and below 20 tonight. Spica, Vega, Arcturus; brilliant. Frost shines on the ground in the light of the setting moon. Very cold, very silent, when I was out during meditation—only a distant train—to have the only one far noise is not equivalent to silence.

8 After the Night Office—cool, and dark—mist on the low bottoms, a glow of red in the east, still a long way from dawn, and small, clear purple clouds in the glow. Sirius shining through the girders of the water tower and high over the building a star travels east—no sound of a plane, perhaps it is some spaceship.

9 A marvelous, clear, clean spring morning: after some warm days and rain yesterday afternoon, the sky is washed of any trace of clouds. The hills in the south stand out sharp against the immaculate morning. Soon the sun will rise. In the most pure silence a pileated woodpecker drums on a loud tree and the solemn sound goes out through the clear halls of the forest.

After five, I looked at the stars, and discerned my zodiacal sign rising in the East, Aquarius, and Venus glittering in Capricorn.

10 The other night in the clear sky about 3:30 suddenly saw in the South the great sign of Scorpio rising. It is awesome to see the T-shaped head climb into the sky and the twisting body slowly follow it up out of Tennessee, with red Antares in its heart!

Seeing this I got out and looked at other constellations with a star map for July. . . . In the west my view is hindered by the tall pine but the sickle and Leo are high and I see them. In the East the beautiful Swan, and the Eagle. Today I went out in the open and could see the Cassiopeia upside down over Boones' in the North.

11 Two nights ago—early morning, before dawn: the old moon—dying crescent—hung in the South with Antares (of Scorpius) almost caught in the crescent. And as if the moon were holding up Scorpius in a balancing act. A forbidding sign. Venus nearby.

12 Last night after a prayer vigil in the novitiate chapel . . . went to bed late at the hermitage. All quiet. No lights at Boone's or Newton's. Cold. Lay in bed realizing that what I was, was happy. Said the strange word "happiness" and realized that it was there, not as an "it" or object. It simply was. And I was that. And this morning, coming down, seeing the multitude of stars above the bare branches of the wood, I was suddenly hit, as it were, with the whole package of meaning of everything: that the immense mercy of God was upon me, that the Lord in infinite kindness had looked down on me and given me this vocation out of love, and that he had always intended this. . . .

13 Before dawn. Red Mars hangs like a tiny artificial fruit from the topmost branch of a bare tree in our *preau*.

14 The shadows fall. The stars appear. The birds begin to sleep. Night embraces the silent half of the earth.

A vagrant, a destitute wanderer with dusty feet, finds his way down a new road. A homeless God, lost in the night, without papers, without identification, without even a number, a frail expendable exile lies down in desolation under the sweet stars of the world and entrusts Himself to sleep.

CHAPTER 5

CREATURES

BUTTERFLIES AND BIRDS

1 Meadowlark sitting quietly on a fence post in the dawn sun, his gold vest—bright in the light of the east, his black bib tidy, turning his head this way, that way. This is a Zen quietness without comment. Yesterday a very small, chic, black and white butterfly on the whitewashed wall of the house.

2 Two white butterflies alight on separate flowers. They rise, play together briefly, accidentally, in the air, they depart in different directions.

3 Receiving an honor:
   A very small gold-winged moth came and settled on the back of my hand, and sat there, so light I could not feel it. I wondered at the beauty and

delicacy of this being—so perfectly made, with mottled golden wings. So perfect. I wonder if there is even a name for it. I never saw such a thing before. It would not go away, until, needing my hand, I blew it lightly into the woods.

In the afternoon: I knew there was an intruder in the front room of the hermitage, where I could hear movement. I went to see, and it was a Carolina wren which had been thinking of coming in already the day before yesterday. It flew out again, as though it were not welcome!

Today it was wonderful. Clouds, sky overcast, but tall streamers of sunlight coming down in a fan over the bare hills.

Suddenly I became aware of great excitement. The pasture was full of birds—starlings. There was an eagle flying over the woods. The crows were all frightened, and were soaring, very high, keeping out of the way. Even more distant still were the buzzards, flying and circling, observing everything from a distance. And the starlings filled every large and small tree, and shone in the light and sang. The eagle attacked a tree full of starlings but before he was near them the whole cloud of them left the tree and avoided him and he came nowhere near them. Then he went away and they all alighted on the ground. They were there moving about and singing for about five minutes. Then, like lightning, it happened. I saw a scare go into the cloud of birds, and they opened their wings and began to rise off the ground and, in that split second, from behind the house and from over my roof a hawk came down like a bullet, and shot straight into the middle of the starlings just as they were getting off the ground. They rose into the air and there was a slight scuffle on the ground as the hawk got his talons into the one bird he had nailed.

It was a terrible and yet beautiful thing, that lightning flight, straight as an arrow, that killed the slowest starling.

Then every tree, every field was cleared. I do not know where all the starlings went. Florida, maybe. The crows were still in sight, but over their wood, their guttural cursing had nothing more to do with this affair. The vultures, lovers of dead things, circled over the bottoms where perhaps there was something dead. The hawk, all alone, in the pasture, possessed his prey. He did not fly away with it like a thief. He stayed in the field like a king with the killed bird, and nothing else came near him. He took his time.

I tried to pray, afterward. But the hawk was eating the bird. And I thought of that flight, coming down like a bullet from the sky behind me and over my roof, the sure aim with which he hit this one bird, as though he had picked it out a mile away. For a moment I envied the lords of the Middle Ages who had their falcons and I thought of the Arabs with their fast horses, hawking on the desert's edge, and I also understood the terrible fact that some men love war. But in the end, I think that hawk is to be studied by saints and contemplatives; because he knows his business. I wish I knew my business as well as he does his.

5 Flycatchers, shaking their wings after the rain.

6 As I was coming back from Dom Frederic's lake, a green heron started up from the water in the culvert under the roadway where all the blackberry bushes are, and flew up into the willows. I could see his beautiful mahogany neck, and his crest was up as he looked back at me. His legs were bright yellow. This was perhaps the same heron I saw the other day at a distance over the night pasture, hardly bigger than a crow.

7 A woodpecker with a cry as sharp as a dagger terrifies the lesser birds, while he is himself benevolent and harmless. The beautiful kingfisher in dazzling flight rattles like a bird of ill omen. So we fear beauty!

8 A white crane standing in sunny water
Briefly shakes herself.
Another flies low over green paddy and alights.

9 Hawk. First the shadow flying downward along
the wall of sunlit foliage. Then the bird itself, trim,
compact substance, in the sky overhead, quite
distinct from woods and trees, flying in freedom.
Barred tail, speckled wings, with sunlight shining
through them. He cut a half circle in emptiness over
the elm. Then he seemed to put his hands in his
pockets and sped, without a wing beat, like a bullet,
to plunge into the grove across the open field.

10 Down there in the wooded hollow full of
cedars I hear a great outcry of bluejays, and yonder
is one of the snipes that are always flying and
ducking around Saint Joseph's hill. In all this I am
reassured by the sweet constant melody of my red
cardinals, who sing their less worldly tunes with no
regard for any other sound on earth. And now the
jays have stopped. Their tribulation rarely lasts very
long.

11 An indigo bunting flies down and grasps the
long, swinging stem of a tiger lily and reaches out,

from them, to eat the dry seed on top of a stalk of grass. A Chinese painting!

12 Eight crows wheel in the sky. An interesting evolution of shadows on the bare hillside beneath them. Sometimes the crows fly low and their dance mingles with the dance of their own shadows on the almost perpendicular olive wall of the mountain pasture. Below, the sighs of the ocean.

13 The calm ocean . . . very blue through the trees. Calla lilies growing wild. A very active flycatcher. The sun shines through his wings as through a Japanese fan. It is the feast of St. Pachomius. Many ferns. A large unfamiliar hawktype bird flew over a little while ago, perhaps a young eagle.

I called Ping Ferry in Santa Barbara last evening. He spoke of birds, of the shore, of Robinson Jeffers and told me the name of the big jay bird all dark with a black crest which I saw yesterday. It is called Stellers Jay. Does the jay know whose bird he is? I doubt it. A marvelous blue!

My piece on the "Wild Places" is to be printed in Center Magazine.

14 Perfectly beautiful spring weather—sky utterly cloudless all day—birds singing all around the hermitage—deep green grass. When I am here, all the time the towhees and tanagers are at peace, not worried, and with their constant singing I always know where they are. It is a wonderful companionship to have them constantly within the very small circle of woods which is their area and mine—where they have their nests and I have mine. Some times the woodthrush comes, but only on special occasions—like the evening of St. Robert's day. Last evening I interrupted my meditation to watch half a dozen savannah sparrows outside my bedroom window.

15 The flycatchers, tamer and tamer, play about the chairs and baskets on my porch right in front of this window. They are enthralling. Wrens come too but less frequently.

16 Thanksgiving very quiet and peaceful, with a little bird I had not noticed before singing, clearly, definitely, seven or eight times (at wide intervals). Re-re-re-mi-mi-do. And with what beautiful finality, as if those three notes contained and summed up all the melodies in the world.

17 In the afternoon, lots of pretty little myrtle warblers were playing and diving for insects in the low pine branches over my head, so close I could almost touch them. I was awed at their loveliness, their quick flight, their hissings and chirpings, the yellow spot on the back revealed in flight, etc. Sense of total kinship with them as if they and I were of the same nature, and as if that nature were nothing but love. And what else but love keeps us all together in being?

18 Last night at dusk, the three tame white ducks went running very fast through the green alfalfa to the river, plunging into the swift waters, swimming to the other side, standing up in the shallows, flapping their white wings. Then the fourth discovered their absence and followed them through another corner of the alfalfa field.

The calls of the crows here in New Mexico as in California, are more muted, more melodious, briefer, less insistent than in the east. The crows seem to be flying at a greater psychic altitude, in a different realm. Yes, of course, a realm of high rocks and stunted piñon pine.

19 A joyful and exciting day, cool, with a great confabulation of crows in the east, and a woodthrush quietly singing in the west.

20 Yesterday—a white eyed vireo playing in the dry sumacs in the hill before you get to the old lake. And a pine warbler in a little elm, standing on his head to get down under the leaves at the end of the branches.

A possum sleeping in the fork of a hickory sapling, with his hand hanging down.

And just now; two little siskins, the tamest things I ever saw, busily working on some dandelions on the ground almost under my feet, where I was reading and walking about below the retaining wall. Lovely birds, very small.

21 Sunday morning. Outside the wall, facing the sheep barn, in the cool morning air—across the blue sky the tracks of a long departed jet plane.

There, in the sycamore to the right, a Carolina wren.

Directly in front, in the willows, a song sparrow.

Over there to the left beyond the cedars a catbird or a mocking bird sings. Yes, a catbird.

22 The warblers are coming through now. Very hard to identify them all, even with field glasses and a bird book. (Have seen at least one that is definitely not in the bird book.) Watching one which I took to be a Tennessee warbler. A beautiful, neat, prim little thing—seeing this beautiful thing which people do not usually see, looking into this world of birds, which is not concerned with us or with our problems. I felt very close to God or felt religious awe anyway. Watching those birds was a food for meditation or a mystical reading. Perhaps better.

Also the beautiful, unidentified red flower or fruit I found on a bud yesterday. I found a bird in the woods yesterday on the feast of St. Francis. Those things say so much more than words.

Mark was saying "The birds don't know they have names."

Watching them I thought: who cares what they are called? But do I have the courage not to care? Why not be like Adam, in a new world of my own, and call them by my own names?

That would still mean that I thought the names were important.

No name and no word to identify the beauty and reality of those birds today, is the gift of God to me in letting me see them.

(And that name—God—is no name! It is like a letter.
X or Y. Yahweh is a better Name—it finally means
Nameless One.)

23 Yesterday afternoon, out by the lake where I
planted the loblolly pines (they are doing well) there
was a small goose in the lake, with some ducks.
Could not identify it by the bird book, but it was
closer to the snow goose than anything else. That
lake was an awfully dangerous place for it! I could
hear the natives whooping in the woods, and gun
shots in the rain.

24 A bright, clear, blue day, warm, but with a
cool wind. Doves and woodpeckers echoing in the
trees, and distant crows, and near flycatchers.

25 A cool evening—or cooler than last evening
and the one before. I am on night watch. It is still
light, though everyone is in bed. A robin still sings in
the garden and tall gold lilies shine in the dusk.

26 After a hot, stuffy weekend, last night there
was a good thundershower and I was glad of the rain,
though I lost some sleep. Today was beautiful as
spring should be, and best of all a couple of quail
start behind the hermitage, and the cock with his trim

black crest whirred off into the pines. I had thought they were all done for.

27 Birds. A titmouse was swinging and playing in the dry weeds by the monastery woodshed. A beautiful, small, trim being. A quail was whistling in the field by the hermitage in the afternoon. What a pure and lovely sound. The sound of perfect innocence.

28 I went out on the porch before dawn to think of these things, and of the words of Ezekiel (22:30). "And I sought among them for a man that might set up a hedge and stand in the gap before me in favor of the land that I might not destroy it, and I found none." And while I was standing there quails began to whistle all over the field and in the wood. I had not heard any for weeks and thought sure they were all dead, for there have been hunters everywhere. No, there they are! Signs of life, of gentleness, of helplessness, of providence, of love. They just keep existing and loving and making more quails and whistling in the bushes.

29 A gang of gray jays flies down into the canyon with plaintive cat-like cries over my head. Some stop to question my presence. They reply to

one another all over the canyon. They would rob me if they thought I had any thing worthwhile. Gray Jay, "Whiskey Jack," a camp robber, inquisitive, versatile (says the bird book).

RAMS AND LAMBS

1 It is quiet. The birds sing and I hear the rams and the lambs and it is the Feast of Saint Anthony of Padua.

2 After None I sat in one of the windows of the Scriptorium, next to a fresh piece of fly-paper that wasn't doing much business, and watched the rain. Out near the big sycamore, where there are usually swine, shorn sheep and lambs were standing in the downpour, about twenty or twenty-five of them I should say. They were all absolutely motionless. Not browsing, not looking about, not considering the slightest change of position. They looked as if they had all been carved out of something. And they were that way for half an hour.

3 Faint cry of a lamb on the mountainside muffled by sea wind.

When I came four or five days ago to Needle Rock, I told the rancher I would be out on this mountainside for a few days. He had just finished shearing. All the sheep were still penned in at the ranch. Now they are all over the mountain again.

This morning I sheltered under a low thick pine while sheep stood bare and mute in the pelting shower.

Song sparrows everywhere in the twisted trees—"neither accept nor reject anything."

(*Astavakra Gita*)

RODENTS AND RABBITS

1 Evening. A turning point in the weather. The heavy rain clouds, broke up a bit this morning. There were few patches of sun, a few short showers late in the afternoon. It is turning cold. I noticed that my woodchuck had buried himself completely, covering up the entrance to his hole, and had gone to sleep for the winter in his bed of leaves. I wish him a happy sleep!

2 (Evening.) Heavy snow all day. Traffic of birds on the porch; juncos first, the cardinals, a mocking bird, titmice, myrtle warblers, etc. Also at least 3

whitefooted mice (pretty with their brown face and big ears) came out of the wood piles—mice more interested than birds in the crumbs. Birds like the shelter and drink from the pools of melted snow.

3 Yesterday I thought it would snow—skies have been grey and even black for over a week. Clouds of birds gathered around the hermitage. Twenty robins or more, a dozen finches, jays, many junkos (including one I found dead on the porch), other small birds and even a couple of bluebirds—I had not seen them around in the winter. Yesterday morning about two I heard something scampering around in the house and found it was a little flying squirrel. I have no idea how he got in. I thought for a moment of keeping him and taming him, but opened the door and turned him loose. At least let the animals be free and be themselves! While they still can.

4 While I was anticipating the night office of St. Mary Magdalen a female tanager captured a grasshopper on the path a few feet away, and after dinner, as I sat under the broad woodshed roof a woodchuck came out of the weeds and chewed at leaves five or six feet away from me, not out of tameness but rather for sheer stupidity. Woodchucks must be shortsighted and depend mostly on hearing, or so I think.

5 A tiny shrew was clinging to the inside of the novitiate screen doors, trapped in the house! I took her up and she ran a little onto my sleeve and then stayed fixed, trembling. I put her down in the grass outside and she ran away free.

6 Yesterday Fr. Anthony and I went out and blessed the fields, starting with the wheat and oats and coming around by St. Bernard's field and Aiden Nally's and across to the bottoms. Out in the calf pasture we blessed some calves who came running up and took a very active interest in everything. Then we blessed pigs, who showed some interest at first. The sheep showed not concern and the chickens ran away as soon as we approached. The rabbits stayed quiet until we threw holy water at them and then they all jumped.

HORSES AND CATTLE

1 I stepped out of the north wing of the monastery and looked out at the pasture where the calves usually are. It was empty of calves. Instead there was a small white colt, running beautifully up the hill, and down, and around again, with a long smooth stride and with the ease of flight. Yet in the middle of

it he would break into rough, delightful cavorting, hurling himself sideways at the wind and the hill, and instantly sliding back into the smooth canter. How beautiful is life this spring!

2 In the afternoon I went out to the old horse barn with the Book of Proverbs and indeed the whole Bible. . . . Afterwards I sat and looked out at the hill and the gray clouds and couldn't read anything. When the flies got too bad I wandered across the bare pasture and sat over by the enclosure wall, perched on the edge of a ruined bathtub that has been placed there for the horses to drink out of. A pipe comes through the wall and plenty of water flows into the bathtub from a spring somewhere in the woods, and I couldn't read there either. I just listened to the clean water flowing and looked at the wreckage of the horsebarn on top of the bare knoll in front of me and remained drugged with happiness and prayer.

Presently the two mares and the two colts came over to see me and to take a drink. The colts looked like children with their big grave eyes, very humble, very stupid and they were tamer than I expected. They came over and nudged me with their soft muzzles and I talked to them for a bit. . . .

Later on I saw other interesting things—for instance a dead possum in a trap and a gold, butter-and-egg butterfly wavering on the dead possum's back. There are many Rhode Island reds over in the southwest corner of the enclosure this year. When I was on retreat for ordination to the priesthood, I galloped to be at work on the roosts we were building for them then.

3 After None drove with Brother Nicholas into the hills behind New Hope, where Edelin has land he may leave to the monastery. A perfect, remote, silent, enclosed valley about two miles deep, wooded, watered by a spring and a creek, no roads; perfect solitude, where there were once two cabins for freed slaves a hundred years ago. Now it is all cattle, a herd of these hundred Herefords and Angus roaming loose in the pasture and the woods and at least two full grown thoroughbred Black Angus bulls, not to mention scores of bull calves. They were quiet though. The silence, the woods, the hills, were perfect. This would be an ideal place for a "desert." . . .

4 Down there, the young bulls sleep behind the single strand of their electric fence.

It is four o'clock in the morning.

5 Sweet afternoon! Cool breezes and a clear sky! This day will not come again.

The bulls lie under the tree in the corner of their field.

Quiet afternoon! The blue hills, the day lilies in the wind. This day will not come again.

SNAKES AND FROGS

1 All the time in the Chama canyon, I was looking out for rattle snakes. It is full of sidewinders. I went gingerly among the rocks and looked everywhere before sitting down. I thought they would like best the heat of the day and the burning rocks, but Denis said they preferred dusk, evening, and the night, yet the nights are cold. In the end, I saw no rattlers except at the zoo in Ghost Ranch Museum. There, a huge ugly monster of a diamondback and three indescribably beautiful others, whose name I forgot—long, lithe, silvery, sandy snakes with neat rattles, lifting up their heads gracefully with swollen sacks of poison. They were too beautiful, too alive, too much themselves to be labeled, still less to have an emotion, fear, admiration, or surprise projected on them. You would meet one in the rocks and hardly see it, for it would be so much like the silver, dead, weathered cedar branches lying

everywhere and exactly the color of sand or a desert vegetation. I understand the Indians' respect for the snake—so different from the attitude ingrained in us since Genesis—our hatred and contempt.

In the desert one does not fight snakes, one simply lives with them and keeps out of their way.

2 Warmer. Rain in the night. Frogs again. At first the waterhole—(four feet long at most) had one frog or two. Now they are a small nation, loud in the night. The innocent nation, chanting blissfully in praise of the spring rain.

3 These quiet hours before and after dawn!

The other day (Thursday)—the *full meaning* of lauds, said against the background of waking birds and sunrise.

At 2:30—no sounds except sometimes a bullfrog. Some mornings, he says Om—some days he is silent. The sounds are not every day the same. The whippoorwill who begins his mysterious whoop about 3 o'clock is not always near. Sometimes, like today, he is very far away in Linton's woods or beyond. Sometimes he is close, on Mount Olivet. Yesterday there were two, but both in the distance.

4 Early mist. Trees of St. Ann's wood barely visible across the valley. A flycatcher, on a fencepost, appears in momentary flight, describes a sudden, indecipherable ideogram against the void of mist, and vanishes. On both sides of the house, the gossip of tangers. The two lizards that operate on the porch scuttle away when I arrive on the porch, however quietly, from outside. But when I come from inside the house, even though I may move brusquely, they are not afraid and stay where they are. To be conscious of both extremes of my solitary life, consolation and desolation; understanding, obscurity; obedience and protest; freedom and imprisonment.

5 There is a small black lizard with a blue, metallic tail, scampering up the yellow wall of the Church next to the niche where the Little Flower, with a confidential and rather pathetic look in her eyes, offers me a rose. I am glad of the distraction because now I can breathe again and think a little.

6 Saturday there was rain at last—after a month or so—and at night, with the rain softly falling, a frog began singing in the waterhole behind the hermitage. Now it sounds as if there are half a dozen of them there, singing their interminable spring celebration.

DEER AND DOGS

1 In the evening, stood for about 15 minutes on the porch watching deer etc. through field glasses. The deer—five of them, were out by the brush piles beyond my fence, barely a hundred yards—less perhaps—from the hermitage. Hence I would see them very clearly and watch all their beautiful movements—from time to time they tried to figure me out, and would spread out their ears at me, and stand still, looking, and there I would be gazing right into those big brown eyes and those black noses. And one, the most suspicious, would lift a foot and set it down again quietly, as if to stomp—but in doubt about whether there was a good reason. This one also had a stylish, high-stepping trot routine which the others did not seem to have. But what form! I was entranced by their perfection!

2 Two nights ago it turned very cold. Yesterday morning as I came down to the monastery in bright,

frozen moonlight, with the hard diamonded leaves crackling under my feet, a deer sprang up in the deep bushes of the hollow. Perhaps two. I could see one in the moonlight.

3 Magenta mist outside the windows. A cock crows over at Boone's. Last evening when the moon was rising saw the warm burning soft red of a doe in the field. It was still light enough so I got the field glasses and watched her. Presently a stag came out, and then I saw a second doe and, briefly, another stag. They were not afraid. Looked at me from time to time. I watched their beautiful running, grazing. Everything, every movement was completely lovely, but there is a kind of gaucheness about them sometimes that makes them even lovelier. The thing that struck me most: one sees, looking at them directly in movement, just what the cave painters saw—something that I have never seen in a photograph. It is an awe-inspiring thing—the *Mantu* or "spirit" shown in the running of the deer, the "deerness" that sums up everything and is sacred and marvelous. A contemplative intuition! Yet perfectly ordinary, everyday seeing. The deer reveals to me something essential in myself! Something beyond the trivialities of my everyday being, and my individuality. The stags much darker, mouse-grey, or rather a warm grey

brown like a flying squirrel. I could sense the softness of their coat and longed to touch them.

4 Came back to the hermitage, not feeling like going to bed. Mist over the field after rain. Diffuse sound of crickets in the dusk. I sat on the porch and the strange owl-like cry of a frightened deer came from the field. I saw the white tail bounding away in the mist. Nine o'clock rings. I had better think of going to bed.

5 Yesterday afternoon it was cold and rainy. . . .

In the evening it cleared, was cold. I came up, sun setting, moon out. I looked out the bedroom window and saw two deer grazing quietly in the field, in dim dusk and moonlight, barely twenty yards from the cottage. Once in a while they would look up at the house with their big ears extended, and even a little movement would make them do this but eventually I walked quietly out on the porch and stayed there and they stayed peacefully until finally I began moving about and they lifted up the white flags of their tails and started off in a wonderful, silent, bounding flight down the field, only to stop a hundred yards away. I don't know what became of them after that, for it was bed time and I had not read my bit of Genesis (Jacob's dream).

6 All day Epiphany I had a sort of emotional hangover from that day in the woods. Sat at the top of the field looking down at the hermitage, tried to meditate sanely in the sun, came out quieter. And cooked myself some supper—a thin potato soup made out of dust in an envelope.

Then as the sun was setting I looked up at the end of the field where I had sat in the afternoon, and suddenly realized that there were beings there—deer. In the evening light they were hard to descry against the tall brown grass, but I could pick out at least five. They stood still looking at me, and I stood looking at them, a lovely moment that stretched into ten minutes perhaps! They did not run (though kids could be heard shouting somewhere down by the waterworks) but eventually walked quietly into the tall grass and bushes and for all I know slept there. When they walked they seemed to multiply so that in the end I thought there must be at least ten of them.

7 Yesterday afternoon, walking about in my own field and in the hollow where the deer sleep, and where a big covey of quail started up in front of me, I saw again how perfect a situation this is, how real, how far beyond my need of comment or justification. All the noises of all the programs, or of all the critics, do nothing to alter this.

8 This morning when I was saying Prime under the pine trees in front of the hermitage, I saw a wounded deer limping along in the field, one leg incapacitated. I was terribly sad at this and began weeping bitterly. And something quite extraordinary happened. I will never forget standing there weeping and looking at the deer standing still looking at me questioningly for a long time, a minute or so. The deer bounded off without any sign of trouble.

9 Today there was a thaw, sunlight, and blueness and warmth in the air. The hills, still snowcovered, were lovely in the haze of the thaw. There were patches on the wet, soft ground, where the snow had melted, and it was good to see the ground. A stray red setter followed me out through the woods, acting as if I were his master, running off, coming back when I stopped and telling me to come on, very pleased when I whistled to him, and acting just like a dog being taken out to run in the woods. In the end, it turned out he had taken me for a walk; led, not followed me, out and back. I wish I could keep him and feed him in my room. How could I ever take care of a dog?

10 *Things nature has been doing while I have been doing what I have been doing:* making that big supple red dog behind the greenhouse grow up out of a small crazy thing that looked like it was going to be a chow. Now it's the prettiest mongrel you ever saw: a big quiet, lithe, gay, red dog with floppy ears, but like a collie, except also like a police dog as to the feet and head. This dog laughs and sings a lot, and talks and jumps up quietly and plays when a guy goes past the greenhouse. I like this dog. That is what nature has been doing, between fall and spring. Last fall when the dog was a pup he got under my feet and got stepped on, accidentally. He does not remember—or if he does, not with malice. I guess he isn't smart enough to know anything. Just playful.

11 Today I walked up on the Two Mile in the new snow that is part of the blizzard that covered New York. It was a wonderful day, with level gray clouds, snow on the hills, woods. The Two Mile is a wonderful road, dipping and turning among small farms lined with spectacular, small trees, and climbing gradually, into the woods, the mountain. It is like mountain country in Germany somewhere.

The shapes of the hillsides are marvelous. Then, along the tops of the hills, the woods of young, straight trees. Icicles on the caves of the small farm houses. Snow, drifted against the black or dark red barns—small barns. The two crazy dogs at one of the farms, one that looked like a fairy-story wolf-bear mixed, who stood up comically on his hind legs when he barked, and knew he was a character in a farce, but tried to be fierce, spoiled it by wagging his tail, got mad at himself, stood up, nearly rolled over backwards. Some vaudeville dog-wolf shaggy in his black coat!

BEES AND BUGS

1 The last three days of Holy Week were beautiful, brilliant days. The finest of all the spring. My redbuds are in bloom and the apple trees are in full bloom down by the monastery beehives. It was wonderful today walking under their great dim clouds full of booming bees.

2 In the few days I have been here trees that were barely budding have now begun to screen the air with greenness of small leaves. Petals are beginning to fall from the apple trees that are crowded with

blossoms—and full of bees filling the sunlight with the sound of their swarming.

Bees are mentioned in today's Mass, too. The Paschal Candle is spoken of as "made from the work of bees"; it is a great honor for the bees to come in such an important place in such an important Mass. I wonder what it signifies.

3 The sun today was as hot as Cuba. Tulips, in the front court, opened their chalices, but widened and became blowsy and bees were working, one in each flower's cup, although it is only April. Fruit trees are in blossom, and every day more and more buds come out on the trees of the great avenue leading to the gate house.

The Trappist brothers in their medieval peasant hoods and their swathed legs and big home-made boots tramp along in a line through the vineyards; bells ring in the steeple.

All the spring which I had looked forward to finding here, from St. Bonaventure's is here, and I haven't been looking at it—for fear of trying to claim I owned it, for fear of taking out title deeds to it, and making it my real estate, as I have everything else. For fear of devouring it like a feast, making it my party,—and so losing it.

4 Here I sit surrounded by bees as I write in this book. The bees are happy and therefore they are silent. They are working in the delicate white flowers of the weeds among which I sit. I am on the east side of the house where I am not as cool as I thought I was going to be, and I sit on top of the bank that looks down over the beehives and the pond where the ducks used to be and Rohan's Knob in the distance. And the big wobbly stepladder I nearly fell off, cleaning the Church once, is abandoned out there at one of the cherry trees, and the branches of a little plum tree before me, right by the road, sag with plums.

5 Nonviolent Himalayan bees: after one had lit on me quietly three times without stinging, I let it crawl on my head a while, picking up sweat for some eclectic and gentle honeycomb, or just picking up sweat for no reason. Another crawled on my hand and I studied it. Certainly a bee. I could not determine whether it was stingless, or just well behaved.

6 Yesterday I killed a big shiny black widow spider in its web, in a rotten tree stump. A beautiful spider, more beautiful than most other species. But I thought I had better kill it, for I nearly sat down next to the stump and someone could get bitten. Strange to be so

close to something that can kill you and not be accompanied by some kind of a "desire"—as if desires were everything. (A car can kill you, too.)

7 Cool morning. The corn is high—over my head already.

A train comes slowly and busily down the valley, whistling first at Dant Station, then New Hope, now Gethsemani, soon New Haven.

A helicopter came over, no better name for it than chopper with its insane racket, insect body, thin tail, half dragonfly half grasshopper *(Sauterelle de l'apocalypse!)* [Grasshopper of the Apocalypse!]. Flew over three times, in a circle around the monastery. What for? Just to make a noise.

8 War on the ants in the hollow and behind the hermitage—millions of them in huge hills. Andy Boone got in to it with whiskey bottles full of kerosene which he sticks upside down into the anthills. But the ants just move and start again five feet away.

9 This is the year of the seventeen year locusts. They are almost silent in the woods now. The woods near at hand are almost entirely quiet. You can hear the locusts faintly in the distant forests. When they first began, about twelve days ago, I thought they

were frogs or crows in the distance. Last week the din was enormous. The whole world throbbed with their love, which had taken over everything. Immense activity in the woods.

When they came out of the ground by the new lake they found the woods had gone which were there 17 (or 18) years ago. But they clustered in the leaves of the low stump sprouts and the suckers and we saw them there, black rubbery bodies, red eyes, and amber wings.

CHAPTER 6

FESTIVALS

RAIN

1 Of course the festival of rain cannot be stopped, even in the city. The woman from the delicatessen scampers along the sidewalk with a newspaper over her head. The streets, suddenly washed, become transparent and alive, and the noise of traffic becomes a plashing of fountains. One would think that the urban man in a rainstorm would have to take account of nature in its wetness and freshness, its baptism and its renewal.

2 We have been praying for rain, and this has been the *imperata* [special prayer] at Mass. So this morning around the offertory a steady rain began (it has been raining on and off for the last thirty-six hours anyway) and it has gone on pouring down ever

135

since, floods of it in a constant and uninterrupted and very vocal cascade all day long. The land is full of its rumor and all our fields have rivers running through them.

3 Fog and rain—close to freezing but not quite.

Pale snow, lavender woods, you cannot see across the valley.

Cleaned up today. Tomorrow is my forty-eighth birthday.

4 The thunder cracks and beats. Rain comes flooding down from the roof eaves and the grass looks twice as green as before.

Not to be known, not to be seen.

5 Let me say this before rain becomes a utility that they can plan and distribute for money. By "they" I mean the people who cannot understand that rain is a festival, who do not appreciate its gratuity, who think that what has no price has no value, that what cannot be sold is not real, so that the only way to make something actual is to place it on the market. The time will come when they will sell you even your rain. At the moment it is still free, and I am in it. I celebrate its gratuity and its meaninglessness.

6 I just looked out of the window into the dark well of a courtyard behind the house. Music from the Baptist church has ceased. The thin rain has not. It falls lightly, cold, crisscrossing in the air. The branches of the tree are stripped absolutely bare: they look like rubber, in the wet.

Water drips on the stones.

I cannot tell if there is still thin unmelted ice in the goldfish pool—or not. Ice pockmarked by the thin cold rain. The snow is all gone.

Over beyond the church, the houses on Eleventh Street—their roofs shine with rain. The sky is black.

I like it when it rains, when the sky is black, when the rain is light and thin. It does not make me feel sad, particularly.

I remember walking along a road toward Caylus with my father. The sky was dark. It was not yet raining, though. The road ran along the top of a ridge, and for a long distance you could see hills, the tops of hills, the gray causses, dry and dotted with white outcrops of rock. When we came upon the valley where Caylus is, the village and its castle, in the gray air, built of gray stone, against the hills, was camouflaged. You could hardly see it for protective coloring.

That was on a Sunday too. We had eaten an omelet at the inn at some little village. When I got home, I probably wrote down in a book about the places we had seen.

7 The rain that I am in is not like the rain of cities. It fills the woods with an immense and confused sound. It covers the flat roof of the cabin and its porch with insistent and controlled rhythms. And I listen, because it reminds me again and again that the whole world turns by rhythms I have not yet learned to recognize, rhythms that are not those of the engineer.

8 Rain all night and a heavy wind out of the South. Buffeting the novitiate chapel during Mass, running headlong into it like a large, soft, live thing, sweeping and brushing all the walls and pounding all the windows. When day came the wind was already gentler and it was good to see all the fields washed with rain and the grass deep in puddles of rain after so many dry weeks.

9 Late afternoon—a good rainstorm began before supper and it is going on now as darkness falls. A moment ago there was a hawk up there flying against the wind in the dark and in the rain, with big black

clouds flying and the pines
bending. A beautiful storm,
and it has filled my buckets
with water for washing, and
the house with cool winds.
It is good and comforting to
sit in a storm with all the winds in the woods outside
and rain on the roof, and sit in a little circle of light
and read and hear the clock tick on the table. And
tomorrow's Gospel is the one about not serving two
Masters, and letting the Lord provide. That is what I
must do.

10 It has been raining steadily for almost 36
hours. This morning toward the end of my meditation
the rain was pouring down on the roof of the
hermitage with great force and the woods resounded
with tons of water falling out of the sky. It was great!
A good beginning for a New Year. Yesterday in a lull
I was looking across the valley at black wet hills,
sharply outlined against the woods, and white
patches of water everywhere in the bottoms: a
landscape well etched by serious weather.

11 I came up here from the monastery last night,
sloshing through the cornfield. . . . The night became
very dark. The rain surrounded the whole cabin with

its enormous virginal myth, a whole world of meaning, of secrecy, of silence, of rumor. Think of it: all that speech pouring down, selling nothing, judging nobody, drenching the thick mulch of dead leaves, soaking the trees, filling the gullies and crannies of the wood with water, washing out the places where men have stripped the hillside! What a thing it is to sit absolutely alone, in the forest, at night, cherished by this wonderful, unintelligible, perfectly innocent speech, the most comforting speech in the world, the talk that rain makes by itself all over the ridges, and the talk of the watercourses everywhere in the hollows!

12 Thunder, lightning and rain all night. Heaviest rain for a long time. Floods in the bottoms. Water bubbling in under the basement wall into the wash room. Novitiate garden flooded in the NW corner. (One day the whole retaining wall will go if this keeps up.) Sound of waters in the valley.

My love is
The fragrance of the orchid
And the sound of waters
says the Haiku on my lovely Zen calendar.

13 During the morning meditation there was a fine thundershower, shaking the whole monastery, floods of rain. All clear by the end of Lauds, and the

day has been bright and hot, but more like May. Away in the south a huge solid cool mountain of cloud over Tennessee.

14 The rain ceases, and a bird's clear song suddenly announces the difference between Heaven and hell.

15 A few drops of rain just started spattering on the leaves, and stopped again. The sky is gray. Birds sing. Far away a bob white exults briefly in the fields where our wheat crop is rotting.

16 There has been no rain for almost three weeks. The woods have been getting very dry. And I have been told of the monotonous succession of bright, hot days walking among the stiff, paper leaves. I have been hoping and praying for rain. So this morning when I went out at dawn and saw the sky dark with clouds I was very happy. The air smelled wet and the pine needles in particular smelled strong and sweet. There may have been a light rain in the night. But at the end of the morning there was a good rain, while I was saying Mass (no server showed up so I said it alone in joy, with pauses where I felt like pausing). Then another good rain in the afternoon after I got back to the hermitage. The musty valley and wet woods filled me with joy.

17 September has come in a great downpour of rain. It began about suppertime last evening and has continued on and off all night. It was especially heavy around 4:15 a.m. when I went out and looked at it and listened to it. Rain creates a double isolation and peace in the hermitage. The noise of it and the thickness of it walls you off from the rest of the world and you know that no one is going to bother to walk up through the woods with all this water coming down.

18 There was a violent thunderstorm about midnight and it went on a long time. Big downpour. This morning, before dawn, misty moon, mist hanging low over the wet fields and bottoms, and a towhee waking in the hedge. Black wet trees against the clouds.

19 Rain in the night, at bedtime. Rain this morning during my early Mass, Mass of Our Lady. At the last Gospel I could see the blue vineyard knob in the grey west with a scapular of mist on it, and then during thanksgiving those other knobs, the pointed one, the woods, of which I never tire. Is it really true that I have no "place"? The little poplar tree I planted on the west side of the chapel in 1957 or '58 is now up to the second floor windows, and I saw great drops

of rain sitting on the fat leaves after the rain had stopped.

20 After two days of wind and rain, a quiet, moonlit night. Fine clouds yesterday evening, piling up black out of the SW, and riding off in a line northward without coming over the monastery. High sweep of pink curves overhead. Then the black descended on us with dark and there was rain.

21 Nobody started it, nobody is going to stop it. It will talk as long as it wants, this rain. As long as it talks I am going to listen.

22 The rain has stopped. The afternoon sun slants through the pine trees: and how those useless needles smell in the clean air!

A dandelion, long out of season, has pushed itself into bloom between the smashed leaves of last summer's day lilies. The valley resounds with totally uninformative talk of creeks and wild water.

Then the quails begin their sweet whistling in the wet bushes. Their noise is absolutely useless, and so is the delight I take in it. There is nothing I would rather hear, not because it is a better noise than other noises, but because it is the voice of the present moment, the present festival.

FLOWERS

1 Gloom and murk of drizzling rain across the valley, more like a cloud than falling rain. What is it full of? But in the twilight day lilies flare discreetly, and poplar leaves turn up in the wind that does not blow this cloud away. It keeps hanging over the valley.

2 The sleet is turning into snow. But my crocuses, in their little tight group, have flourished bravely two weeks since Ash Wednesday even in snow and some very cold weather.

3 The gardenias, of which there have been plenty, are running out. But now one stands before the face of this Angel on the cover of the new Rublev book which came today from Bob Rambusch.

One of the fairest gardenias was a large one which I picked for Our Lady on her feast of Mt. Carmel, and it had raindrops on it which stayed most of the morning.

4 Now a beautiful yellow rose bush has filled with flowers. They stand before me like something very precious in the late slanting sun as I write.

5 The crocuses multiply and are still there after nearly a month, with some very cold weather. Bees in them yesterday. I walked in the woods. Woods ringing with distant voices. . . .

6 Yesterday all day that small gardenia was a great consolation. Since it rained I stayed in and wrote. . . .

But I stayed long looking at a goldfinch and walked slowly up through the woods, gazing at the tall straight oaks that are before you reach the stile. Everything is beautiful and I am grateful for all of it. And maybe now I begin to be old, and walk slowly, like Victor Hammer.

When the Dalai Lama was young, still a boy, he was lonely in the Potala and would walk on the roof looking through field glasses down upon the houses of his subjects to see if they were having parties and to watch their enjoyment. But they in turn would hide themselves so as not to sadden him still more.

7 Yesterday beautiful, cool after violent storms. . . . Sat in the cool woods, bare feet in the wet grass, and my quails whirling near me for my comfort, and wrote a poem about a flower.

8 The little locust tree by the corner of the wall has died and spilled all the fragments of its white flowers over the ground until that part of the garden looks like a picture by Seurat.

9 Flowers at Bear Harbor. Besides wild irises three or four feet high, there are callalilies growing wild among the ferns and the strange bank . . . and a profusion of roses and a lot of flowering shrubs that I cannot name.

10 Beauty of the sunlight falling on a tall vase of red and white carnations and green leaves on the altar in the novitiate chapel. The light and shade of the red, especially the darkness in the fresh crinkled flower and the light warm red around the darkness, the same color as blood but not "red as blood," utterly unlike blood. Red as a carnation. This flower, this light, this moment, this silence = *Dominus est* [the Lord is here], eternity! Best because the flower is itself and the light is itself and the silence is itself and I am myself—all, perhaps, an illusion but no matter, for illusion is nevertheless shadow of reality and reality is the grace that under lays these lights, these colors, and this silence.

TREES

1 The wrens built their nest last week.

The linden leaves are beginning to come out and this week we will see beech leaves, which are the loveliest things in creation when they are just unfolding.

2 Driving down through the redwoods was indescribably beautiful along Eel River. There is one long stretch where the big trees have been protected and saved—like a completely primeval forest. Everything from the big ferns at the base of the trees, the dense undergrowth, the long enormous shafts towering endlessly in shadow penetrated here and there by light. A most moving place—like a cathedral. I kept thinking of the notes of Francis Ponge on the fir forest of Central France. But what could one say about these?

3 I now realize that when John Paul was here last week it was very pretty. Especially coming over the hill and down that valley into Chipmunk. The road down that valley is more mountainous than any around here, a lot of crazy turns, and big drops over the rock talus down among the oil wells and the trees. Wild cherry trees were out everywhere,

covered with, like a powder, green white little blossoms. Like greenish white smoke.

But now the apple trees are out. The other day I was walking past the greenhouse. The sun drowned in the apple tree. The greenhouse looked like a big aquarium tank, all around in the breeze, petals of apple blossoms snowed down and fell noiseless on the fresh, damp, very green, new mowed grass. Now I write about it not terrifically fast, but fast enough so that my hand aches.

4 We do not realize that the fields and the trees have fought and still fight for their respective places on this map—which, by natural right, belong entirely to the trees. We do not remember that these little clumps and groves are the fifth column of the aboriginal forest that wants to return. It is nice to think of, for a moment. But what could be more desperate than a journey, mile after mile, without hills, as rough as all those trees, and never know where you are going. But now it is wide open.

I do not commit myself, though. I am perhaps still on the side of the trees.

5 Climbing to the top of the high ridge before the sea: tall firs reaching into the sun above smokes, mists. Then down into the ferns!

6 How slender are the bodies of the young black oaks! With one stroke of the brush you could make them beautiful, on paper, but that would never be what they are.

The sun suddenly touches the woods beyond the cornfield, rapidly washes the hillside with a little pale light. Everything else is dark and wet, for the air is so wet you can swim in it.

7 The beauty of the walnut tree at the end of the novitiate wall. More beautiful still because of the dead end of the branches that reach out, stark and black, from the rich foliage and gesture against the sky and the hills. The great leaves and the innumerable shades and patterns where they overlap. Inexhaustible beauty of design, made more curious and fecund by the pruning two years ago that was not quite successful.

8 Wet snow and heavy ice bows down all the evergreens and I am afraid of it ruining the loblolly pine sapling in the garden—I am attached to it.

9 The worshipful cold spring light on the sandbanks of Eel River, the immense silent redwoods. Who can see such trees and bear to be away from

them? I must go back. It is not right that I should die under lesser trees.

10 I return to the small locust, whose slow dance in the wind is like that of a Japanese dancer—she turns up her delicate branches in the wind and the undersides of the leaves smile at the sun.

P R E S E N C E S

M O U N T A I N S

1 On the last day of January 1915, under the sign of the Water Bearer, in a year of a great war, and down in the shadow of some French mountains, I came into the world.

2 "Oh! Since I was a baby in the Pyrenees,
   when old St. Martin marked me for the cloister from high Canigou."

3 Very hot. The birds sing and the monks sweat and about 3:15, when I had just changed all our clothes for the fourth time today and hung out the wet ones to dry, I stood in the doorway of the grand parlor and looked at a huge pile of Kentucky cumulus cloud out beyond Mount Olivet—with a

buzzard lazily planing back and forth over the sheep pasture, very high and black against the white mountain of cloud. Blue shadows on the cloud.

4 Snow-covered mountains. Thirty-nine thousand feet over Idaho. Frozen lakes. Not a house, not a road. Gulfs. No announcement. Hidden again.

We are all secrets. But now, where there are suggested gaps, one can divine rocks and snow. "Be a mountain diviner!"

5 The new consciousness.

Reading the calligraphy of snow and rock from the air.

A sign of snow on a mountainside as if my own ancestors were hailing me.

We bump. We burst into secrets.

6 Blue-shadowed mountains and woods under the cloud, then tiny shinings, tin-roofed houses at a crossroad. An olive-green valley floor. A low ridge thinly picked out at the very top in blown snow. The rest, deep green. One of the most lovely

calligraphies I have ever seen. Distant inscaped mountains and near flat lowland. A scrawl of long fire. Smoke a mile or two long. Then a brown rich-veined river. A four-lane super highway with nothing on it.

7 Two volcanoes: *Iliamna* mysterious, feminine, akin to the great Mexican volcanoes. A volcano to which one speaks with reverence, lovely in the distance, standing above the sea of clouds. Lovely near at hand with smaller attendant peaks. *Redoubt* (which surely has another name, a secret and true name) handsome and noble in the distance, but ugly, sinister as you get near it. A brute of a dirty busted mountain that has exploded too often. A bear of a mountain. A dog mountain with steam curling up out of the snow crater. As the plane drew near there was turbulence and we felt the plane might at any moment be suddenly pulled out of its course and hurled against the mountain. As if it would not pull itself away. But finally it did. *Redoubt*. A volcano to which one says nothing.

8 It was quiet flying to Eureka yesterday afternoon in a half-empty plane. One jet flight a day to this forgotten lumber town. Distant presences of Lassen peak and Mount Shasta, especially Shasta . . . like great silent Mexican gods, white and solemn. Massively suspended alone, over haze and over thousands of lower ridges.

9 Eight crows wheel in the sky. An interesting evolution of shadows on the bare hillside beneath them. Sometimes the crows fly low and their dance mingles with the dance of their own shadows on the almost perpendicular olive wall of the mountain pasture. Below, the sighs of the ocean.

10 Sangre de Cristo Mountains, blue and snowy. But after Santa Fe, marvelous long line of snowless, arid mountains, clean long shapes stretching for miles under pure light. Mesas, full rivers, cotton woods, sage brush, high red cliffs, piñon pines. Most impressed of all by the miles of emptiness.

11 The curvature of space around Mount Analogue makes it possible for people to live as though Mount Analogue did not exist. Hence, everyone comes from an unknown country and almost everyone from a too well known country.

12 First sight of mountains in Alaska, strongly ribbed, through clouds. Superb blue of the gulf, indescribable ice patterns. Bird wings, vast mottled, long black streamers, curves, scimitars, lyre bird tails.

13 This afternoon—in the sun at the foot of a birch, in the bushes near the monastery at a point where you can see Mt. McKinley and Mt. Foraker—great, silent and beautiful presence in the afternoon sun.

14 I dreamt I was lost in a great city and was walking "toward the center" without quite knowing where I was going. Suddenly I came to a dead end, but on a height, looking at a great bay, an arm of the harbor I saw a whole section of the city spread out before me on hills covered with light snow, and realized that, though I had far to go, I knew where I was: because in this city there are two arms of the harbor and they help you to find your way, as you are always encountering them.

15 Most impressive mountains I've seen in Alaska: Drum and Wrangell and the third great massive one whose name I forget, rising out of the vast birchy plain of Copper Valley. They are sacred and majestic mountains, ominous, enormous, noble, stirring. You want to attend to them. I could not keep my eyes off them. Beauty and terror of the Chugach. Dangerous valleys. Points. Saws. Snowy nails.

16 . . . all of a sudden I looked out and there were the Himalayas—several hundred miles away,

but an awesome, great white wall of the highest mountains I have ever seen. I recognized the highest ones in the group, though not individually. Everest and Kanchenjunga were in the distance. Later a big, massive one stood out but I did not know what it was. And the river Ganges.

17 In the afternoon I got my first real taste of the Himalayas. I climbed a road out of the village up into the mountains, winding through pines, past places where Tibetans live and work. . . . Many Tibetans on the road, and some were at work on a house, singing their building song. Finally I was out alone in the pines, watching the clouds clear from the medium peaks—but not the high snowy ones—and the place was filled with a special majestic kind of mountain silence. At one point the sound of a goatherd's flute drifted up from a pasture below. An unforgettable valley with a river winding at the bottom, a couple of thousand feet below, and the rugged peaks above me, and pines twisted as in Chinese paintings. I got on a little path where I met at least five Tibetans silently praying with rosaries in their hands—and building little piles of stones. . . . Great silence of the mountain. . . . Gradually the clouds thinned before one of the higher peaks, but it never fully appeared.

18 Yesterday as I came down the path from the mountain I heard a strange humming behind me. A Tibetan came by quietly droning a monotonous sound, a prolonged "*om.*" It was something that harmonized with the mountain—an ancient syllable he had found long ago in the rocks—or perhaps it had been born with him.

19 Last night I had a curious dream about Kanchenjunga. I was looking at the mountain and it was pure white, absolutely pure, especially the peaks that lie to the west. And I saw the pure beauty of their shape and outline, all in white. And I heard a voice saying—or got the clear idea of: "There is an other side to the mountain." I realized that it was turned around and every thing was lined up differently; I was seeing from the Tibetan side. This morning my quarrel with the mountain is ended. Not that it is a big love affair—but why get mad at a mountain? It is beautiful, chastely white in the morning sun—and right in view of the bungalow window.

20 There is another side of Kanchenjunga and of every mountain—the side that has never been photographed and turned into postcards. That is the only side worth seeing.

Out on the mountainside in the warm sun there is the sound of an ax where someone splits wood for fuel at the tea factory. Some children are playing in the same place high up on the edge of the woods. Far below, the lovely blue veil of a woman walking with children along a winding path through a tea garden.

21 Later: I took three more photos of the mountain. An act of reconciliation? No, a camera cannot reconcile one with anything. Nor can it see a real mountain. The camera does not know what it takes: it captures materials with which you reconstruct not so much what you saw as what you thought you saw. Hence the best photography is aware, mindful, of illusion and uses illusion, permitting and encouraging it—especially unconscious and powerful illusions that are not normally admitted on the scene.

22 Kanchenjunga this afternoon. The clouds of the morning parted slightly and the mountain, the massif of attendant peaks, put on a great, slow, silent dance of snow and mist, light and shadow, surface and sinew, sudden cloud towers spiraling up out of icy holes, blue expanses of half-revealed rock, peaks appearing and disappearing with the top of Kanchenjunga remaining the visible and constant

president over the whole slow show. It went on for hours. Very stately and beautiful. Then toward evening the clouds cleared some more, except for a long apron of mist and shadow below the main peaks. There were a few discreet showings of whorehouse pink but most of it was shape and line and shadow and form. O Tantric Mother Mountain! Yin-yang palace of opposites in unity! Palace of *anicca*, impermanence and patience, solidity and nonbeing, existence and wisdom. A great consent to be and not-be, a compact to delude no one who does not first want to be deluded. The full beauty of the mountain is not seen until you too consent to the impossible paradox: it is and is not. When nothing more needs to be said, the smoke of ideas clears, the mountain is SEEN.

23 When you begin each day by describing the look of the same mountain, you are living in the grip of delusion. Today the peak of Kanchenjunga was hidden by massive clouds, but the lower attendant peaks stood out all the more beautiful and noble in their own right. If Kanchenjunga were not there they would all be great mountains on their own. At the end of the line I noticed one that seemed to have had its top cut off, and as I had not noticed anything before I concluded that this beheading had taken place during the night.

CHAPTER 8

SANCTUARY

FOREST

1 My Zen is in the slow swinging tops of sixteen pine trees.

One long thin pole of a tree fifty feet high swings in a wider arc than all the others and swings even when they are still.

Hundreds of little elms springing up out of the dry ground under the pines.

My watch lies among oak leaves. My tee shirt hangs on the barbed wire fence, and the wind sings in the bare wood.

2 Out here in the woods I can think of nothing except God and it is not so much that I think of Him either. I am as aware of Him as of the sun and the clouds and the blue sky and the thin cedar trees. When

I first came out here, I was asleep . . . but I read a few lines from the Desert Fathers and then, after that, my whole being was full of serenity and vigilance.

Who am I writing this for, anyway! It is a waste of time! Enough to say that as long as I am out here I cannot think of Camaldoli either; no question of being here and dreaming of somewhere else. Engulfed in the simple and lucid actuality which is the afternoon: I mean God's afternoon, this sacramental moment of time when the shadows will get longer and longer, and one small bird sings quietly in the cedars, and one car goes by in the remote distance and the oak leaves move in the wind.

3 And now in the woods, I once again revisit the idea of simply staying here, in the woods—with great interior freedom, and applying myself to the main business, which has nothing to do with places, and does not require a beach of pure, white Caribbean sand. Only silence and a curtain of trees.

4 All around us, the steep hills were thick with woods, small gnarled oaks, clinging to the rock. Along the river, the slender poplars rippled with the light of the afternoon, and green waters danced on stones.

5 To go out to walk silently in this wood—this is a more important and significant means to understanding, at the moment, than a lot of analysis and a lot of reporting on the things "of the spirit."

6 Yesterday morning (Sunday) I went to Reverend Father and we were talking about solitude, and quite by surprise he gave me permission to go out of the enclosure into the woods by myself. And so I took advantage of it in the afternoon, although there was a wall of black sky beyond the knobs to the west, and you could hear thunder growling all the time in the distance. It was very hot and damp but there was a good wind coming from the direction of the storm. . . .

First I stopped under an oak tree on top of the hill behind Nally's and sat there looking out at the wide sweep of the valley and the miles of flat woods over toward the straight-line of the horizon where Rohan's knob is.

As soon as I get away from people the Presence of God invades me. And when I am not divided by being with strangers (in a sense anyone I live with will always remain a stranger), I am with Christ.

The wind ran over the bent, brown grasses and moved the shoulders of all the green trees, and I looked at the dark green mass of woods beyond the distillery on those hills down to the south of us and realized that it is when I am with people that I am lonely and when I am alone I am no longer lonely because then I have God and converse with Him (without words) without distraction or interference. Like the man in Ramón Llull who was meditating on the hill, and a stranger came to him and said, "Why are you alone?" And he answered, "You are right in saying I am alone. Before you came I was not alone, but now you are here with me and I am alone indeed."

I thought, if it rains, I will have to go back to the monastery.

Gethsemani looked beautiful from the hill. It made much more sense in its surroundings. We do not realize our own setting and we ought to: it is important to know where you are put on the face of the earth. Physically, the monastery is in a splendid solitude. There is nothing to complain about from the point of view of geography. One or two houses a mile and a half away and the woods and pastures and bottoms and cornfields and hills for miles and miles. And we huddle together in the midst of it and jostle one another like a subway crowd and deafen ourselves with our own typewriters and tractors. . . .

And I thought: if we only knew how to *use* this space and this area of sky and these free woods.

Then the Spirit of God got hold of me and I started
through the woods. I used to be afraid of lightning
before I came to the monastery. Now there didn't
seem to be any particular objection to walking right
into the storm although behind me was the big field
where two boys were killed by lightning last summer
or the one before. . . .

I had a vague idea that there was a nice place
beyond the field we call Hick's House, although
there has been no house there for years. I went to the
calf-pasture beyond St. Malachy's field at the foot of
the knob where the real woods begin. It is a sort of
cova where Our Lady might appear. . . .

And I thought—"Nobody ever comes here!" The
marvelous quiet! The sweet scent of the woods—the
clean stream, the peace, the inviolate solitude! And
to think that no one pays any attention to it. It is there
and we despise it, and we never taste anything like it
with our fuss and our books, our sign-language and
our tractors and our broken-down choir.

One moment of that quiet washed clean the deep,
dark inward mirror of my soul and everything inside
me was swamped in a prayer that could not be quite
pure because there was necessarily so much natural
exultation. There was smoke in it, but I had to accept
that, and there wasn't much I could do about it
because, anyway, I am full of grime.

To say I was happy is to say how far short the
prayer was of perfection, but I was consciously and

definitely and swimmingly happy, and I wonder how I ever stayed on the ground at all. The black clouds meanwhile piled up over the glen, and I went to where there was a shed, down at the entrance to the wilderness, a shed for the calves to shelter in cold weather in the fall.

Yet it did not rain.

I looked up at the pines and at the black smoke boiling in the sky and nothing could make that glen less wonderful, less peaceful, less of a house of joy.

When I finally decided it would soon be time for Vespers, I started back for the monastery the long-way round, keeping a screen of woods between me and the house so that I would not hit the road any-where near where I might be seen from the back of the house where the monks were. I got in just after the first bell for Vespers and only when we were in choir for first Vespers of the Feast of the Sacred Heart did it begin to

rain. Even then it did not rain much. On my way
home I turned to the storm and saw it was marching
northeastward following the line of the knobs, over
on the other side of them, following the line of the
Green River turnpike that is far over there beyond our
property in the woods, going from New Haven to
Bardstown.

I don't know what light this all throws on my
vocation. I do not understand. Last night in my
imperfection, I came out of meditation with a wild
scheme for starting a sort of Carmelite Desert out there.
I know I'd never be allowed a one-man hermitage, but
perhaps one might start a little house for special
retreats, where Priors and Guestmasters and what not
could escape for a little recollection. Where one could
go for a month at a time or even more and get in some
real and solid contemplation. . . .

One thing I must say: both in the wood and
especially on my way back, crossing an open hillock,
all that I had tasted in solitude seemed to have a
luminously intelligible connection with the Mass. It
seemed to be a function or an expression of that
morning's offertory and of the next day's—the Feast's.
It seemed to be, in my own very personal instance,
the very heart of the Feast of Christ's Heart, its clear
manifestation to me. It seemed to clarify and express
in an ineffable way my identification with Christ in
the Mass, and my prayer in the wood was eminently

the prayer of a priest, so that I wonder if my eyes have been momentarily opened and if what I have seen is really more than a poetic intuition—really something that could put in a claim to deeper and more directive significance. Could I end up as something of a hermit-priest, of a priest of the woods or the deserts or the hills, devoted to a Mass of pure adoration that would put all nature on my paten in the morning and praise God more explicitly with the birds?

7 The quiet of the long afternoon of Holy Week. Yesterday I burned some brush in the woods near the hermitage. I love the woods, particularly around the hermitage. Know every tree, every animal, every bird. Sense of relatedness to my environment—a luxury I refuse to renounce. Aristocrat, conservative: I don't give a damn. Those city Christians can live in their world of Muzak and CO_2 and think they are in touch with "creation"—nature "humanism"! I admit that it is a reality one must acknowledge but am not so sure it is better for self-confrontation.

8 From "Day of a Stranger" *
The hills are blue and hot: There is a brown, dusty field in the bottom of the valley. I hear a machine, a bird, a clock. The clouds are high and enormous. In them, the inevitable jet plane passes: this time

probably full of fat passengers from Miami to Chicago, but presently it will be a plane with the bomb in it. I have seen the plane with the bomb in it fly low over me and I have looked up out of the woods directly at the closed bay. Like everyone else I live under the bomb. But unlike most people I live in the woods. Do not ask me to explain this. I am embarrassed to describe it. I live in the woods out of necessity. I am both a prisoner and an escaped prisoner. I can not tell you why, born in France, my journey ended here. I have tried to go further but I cannot. It makes no difference. When you are beginning to be old, and I am beginning to be old, for I am fifty; both times and places no longer take on the same meaning. Do I have a "day"? Do I spend my "day" in a "place"? I know there are trees here. I know there are birds here. I know the birds in fact very well, for there are exactly fifteen pairs of birds living in the immediate area of my cabin and I share this particular place with them: we form an ecological balance. This harmony gives "place" a different configuration. As to crows, they form part of a different pattern. They are vociferous and self-justifying, like humans.

But there is a mental ecology too, a living balance of spirits in this corner of woods. There is a place for many other songs besides those of birds. Of Vallejo for instance. Or the dry, disconcerting voice of Nicanor

Parra (who certainly does not waste his time justifying anything). Sometimes at four o'clock on a very dark cold morning I have sat alone in the house with the rain beating down on it, with a big cup of hot black coffee, translating some poems of Nicanor Parra. Or there is also Chuang Tzu, whose climate is perhaps most the climate of this hot corner of the woods. A climate in which there is no need for explanations. There is also a Syrian hermit called Philoxenus. There is the clanging prose of Tertullian. There is the deep vegetation of that more ancient forest than mine: the deep forest in which the great birds Isaias and Jeremias sing. When I am most sickened by the things that are done by the country that surrounds this place I will take out the prophets and sing them in loud Latin across the hills and send their fiery words sailing south over the mountains to the place where they split atoms for the bombs in Tennessee.

There is also the non-ecology, the destructive unbalance of nature, poisoned and unsettled by bombs, by fallout, by exploitation: the land ruined, the waters contaminated, the soil charged with chemicals, ravaged with machinery, the houses of farmers falling apart because everybody goes to the city and stays there. . . . There is no poverty so great as that of the prosperous, no wretchedness so dismal as affluence. Wealth is poison. There is no misery to compare with that which exists where technology has been a total success. I know these are hard sayings, and that they are unbearable when they are said in other countries where so many lack everything. But do you imagine that if you become as prosperous as the United States you will no longer have needs? Here the needs are even greater. Full bellies have not brought peace and satisfaction but dementia, and in any case not all the bellies are full either. But the dementia is the same for all.

I live in the woods out of necessity. I get out of bed in the middle of the night because it is imperative that I hear the silence of the night, alone, and, with my face on the floor, say psalms, alone, in the silence of the night.

It is necessary for me to live here alone without a woman, for the silence of the forest is my bride and the sweet dark warmth of the whole world is my love, and out of the heart of that dark warmth comes the secret that is heard only in silence, but it is the root of all the secrets that are whispered by all the lovers in their beds all over the world. I have an obligation to preserve the stillness, the silence, the poverty, the virginal point of pure nothingness which is at the center of all other loves. I cultivate this plant silently in the middle of the night and water it with psalms and prophecies in silence. It becomes the most beautiful of all the trees in the garden, at once the primordial paradise tree, the axis mundi, the cosmic axle, and the Cross. *Nulla silva talem profert* [No tree brings forth such].

It is necessary for me to see the first point of light which begins to be dawn. It is necessary to be present alone at the resurrection of Day, in the solemn silence at which the sun appears, for at this moment all the affairs of cities, of governments, of war departments, are seen to be the bickerings of mice. I receive from the Eastern woods, the tall oaks, the one word DAY, which is never the same. It is always in a totally new language.

After dawn I go down into the valley, first under the pines, then under tall oaks, then down a sharp incline, past an old barn, out into the field where they are now planting corn. Later in the summer the corn will be tall and sacred and the wind will whisper through the thousands of leaves and stalks as if all the spirits of the Maya were there. I weep in the corn for what was done in past ages, in the carnage that brought America the dignity of having a "history." I live alone with the blood of Indians on my head.

The long yellow side of the monastery faces the sun on a sharp rise with fruit trees and beehives. I climb sweating into the novitiate, put down my water bottle on the cement floor. The bell is ringing. I have some duties in the monastery. When I have accomplished these, I return to the woods. In the choir are the young monks, patient, serene, with very clear eyes, thin, reflective, gentle. For fifteen years I have given them classes, these young ones who come, and grow thin, become more reflective, more silent. But many of them become concerned with questions. Questions of liturgy, questions of psychology, questions of history. Are they the right questions? In the woods there are other questions and other answers, for in the woods the whole world is naked and directly present, with no monastery to veil it.

Chanting the alleluia in the second mode: strength and solidity of the Latin, seriousness of the second mode, built on the Re as though on a sacrament, a presence. One keeps returning to the Re as to an inevitable center. Sol-Re, Fa-Re, Sol-Re, Do-Re. Many other notes in between, but suddenly one hears only the one note. *Consonantia* [harmony] all notes, in their perfect distinctness, are yet blended in one. . . .

In the heat of noon I return through the cornfield, past the barn under the oaks, up the hill, under the pines, to the hot cabin. Larks rise out of the long grass singing. A bumblebee hums under the wide shady eaves.

I sit in the cool back room, where words cease to resound, where all meanings are absorbed in the *consonantia* of heat, fragrant pine, quiet wind, bird song and one central tonic note that is unheard and unuttered. Not the meditation of books, or of pieties, or of systematic trifles. In the silence of the afternoon all is present and all is inscrutable. One central tonic note to which every other sound ascends or descends, to which every other meaning aspires, in order to find its true fulfillment. To ask when the note will sound is to lose the afternoon: it has sounded and all things now hum with resonance of its sounding.

I sweep. I spread a blanket out in the sun. I cut grass behind the cabin. Soon I will bring the blanket in again and make the bed. The sun is over clouded. Perhaps there will be rain. A bell rings in the monastery. A tractor growls in the valley. Soon I will cut bread, eat supper, say psalms, sit in the back room as the sun sets, as the birds sing outside the window, as silence descends on the valley, as night descends. As night descends on a nation intent upon ruin, upon destruction, blind, deaf to protest, crafty, powerful, unintelligent. It is necessary to be alone, to be not part of this, to be in the exile of silence, to be in a manner of speaking a political prisoner. No matter where in the world he may be, no matter what may be his power of protest, or his means of expression, the poet finds himself ultimately where I am. Alone, silent, with the obligation of being very careful not to say what he does not mean, not to let himself be persuaded to say merely what another wants him to say, not to say what his own past work has led others to expect him to say.

The poet has to be free from everyone else, and first of all from himself, because it is through this "self" that he is captured by others. Freedom is found under the dark tree that springs up in the center of the night and of silence, the paradise tree, the axis mundi, which is also the Cross.

*Merton was asked by his friend Miguel Grinberg in Buenos Aires for some journal passages that would describe a "typical day" in his life and that could be published in the periodical he edited, *Eco Contemporaneo.* Merton responded by writing a "journal-like" essay, which he called "Day of a Stranger." This is the first draft of "Day of a Stranger"; Merton later revised and expanded the essay.

Trinity Sunday after the Night Office I realized I had plenty of time to go to the hermitage and went as the sun rose. I wonder why I had not thought of it before—perhaps too obsessed with the reading I have been doing at that time, and in which to a great extent I have been fruitlessly lost.

This morning I came up again, and I am doing my best to take, as far as possible, the whole day here, going down of course for exercises. Which is possible, as I have no conference or direction.

This morning at four. Great full moon over Nally's hill, pale and clear. A faint mist hanging over the wet grass of the bottoms.

More and more I appreciate the beauty and solemnity of the "Way" up through the woods, past the bull barn, up the stony rise, into the grove of tall, straight oaks and hickories, and around through the pines on top of the hill, to the cottage.

Sunrise. Hidden by pines and cedars on the east side of the house. Saw the red flame of it glaring through the cedars not like sunrise but like a forest fire. From the window of the front room, then, he, the Sun (can hardly be conceived as other than he) shone silently with solemn power through the pine branches.

Now after High Mass the whole valley is glorious with morning, and with the song of birds.

It is essential to experience all the times and moods of this place. No one will know or be able to say *how* essential. Almost the first and most important element of a truly spiritual life, lost in the constant, formal routine of Divine offices under the fluorescent lights in choir— practically no change between night and day.

10 Why do I live alone? I don't know. . . . In some mysterious way I am condemned to it. . . . I cannot have enough of the hours of silence when nothing happens. When the clouds go by. When the trees say nothing. When the birds sing. I am completely addicted to the realization that just being there is enough, and to add something else is to mess it all up. It would be so much more wonderful to be all tied up in someone . . . and I know inexorably that this is not for me. It is a kind of life from which I am absolutely excluded. I can't desire it. I can only desire this absurd business of trees that say nothing, of birds that sing, of a field in which nothing ever happens (except perhaps that a fox comes and plays, or a deer passes by). This is crazy. It is lamentable. I am flawed, I am nuts. I can't help it. Here I am, now, . . . happy as a coot. The whole business of saying I am flawed is a lie. I am happy. I cannot explain it. . . . Freedom, darling. This is what the woods mean to me. I am free, free, a wild being, and that is all that I ever can really be. I am dedicated to it, addicted to it, sworn to it, and sold to it. It is the freedom in me that loves you. . . .

Darling, I am telling you: this life in the woods is IT. It is the only way. It is the way everybody has lost. . . . It is life, this thing in the woods. I do not claim it is real. All I say is that it is the life that has chosen itself for me.

A Midsummer Diary for M. June 23, 1966

S O P H I A

There is in all visible things an invisible fecundity, a dimmed light, a meek namelessness, a hidden wholeness. This mysterious Unity and Integrity is Wisdom, the Mother of all, *Natura naturans.* There is in all things an inexhaustible sweetness and purity, a silence that is a fount of action and joy. It rises up in wordless gentleness and flows out to me from the unseen roots of all created being, welcoming me tenderly, saluting me with indescribable humility. This is at once my own being, my own nature, and the Gift of my Creator's Thought and Art within me, speaking as Hagia Sophia, speaking as my sister, Wisdom.

I am awakened, I am born again at the voice of this my Sister, sent to me from the depths of the divine fecundity.

—"Hagia Sophia,"
Emblems of a Season of Fury, p. 61

NOTES

ABBREVIATIONS

Chapter 1 "To Know Living Things"
1. *RU*, pp. 7-8
2. *SJ*, p. 321
3. *SS*, pp. 189-190
4. *TTW*, pp. 299-300
5. *TTW*, p. 312
6. *TTW*, p. 312
7. *SS*, p. 111
8. *SS*, p. 45
9. *HR*, p. 40
10. *NSC*, pp. 30-31
11. *DWL*, p. 319, #127
12. *TTW*, p. 123
13. *DWL*, p. 227
14. *DWL*, p. 229
15. *ES*, pp. 215-216

Chapter 2 Seasons
Autumn
1. *RTM*, pp. 68-69
2. *TTW*, p. 260
3. *DWL*, p. 308
4. *TTW*, p. 257
5. *OSM*, p. 177
6. *RTM*, p. 238
7. *DWL*, pp. 3-4

Winter
1. *ES*, p. 257
2. *DWL*, p. 172
3. *VC*, p. 25
4. *CGB*, pp. 148-149
5. *OSM*, p. 33
6. *OSM*, p. 32
7. *OSM*, p. 37
8. *OSM*, p. 60
9. *DWL*, p. 52
10. *DWL*, p. 52
11. *LL*, p. 24
12. *DWL*, p. 168
13. *OSM*, p. 94
14. *SJ*, p. 280

Spring
1. *CGB*, p. 285
2. *DWL*, p. 99
3. *LL*, p. 19
4. *OSM*, p. 64
5. *TTW*, p. 311
6. *OSM*, p. 81
7. *OSM*, p. 84
8. *RU*, p. 106
9. *CGB*, p. 132
10. *SS*, pp. 196-197
11. *DWL*, p. 216
12. *TTW*, p. 300
13. *RTM*, p. 5

Summer
1. *SJ*, p. 107
2. *CGB*, p. 45
3. *TTW*, p. 346
4. *DWL*, p. 254
5. *TTW*, p. 237
6. *SJ*, pp. 61-62

Chapter 3 Elements
Earth
1. *ES*, pp. 4-5
2. *TTW*, p. 106
3. *SJ*, pp. 263-264
4. *SJ*, p. 264
5. *SJ*, p. 69
6. *OSM*, p. 167
7. *DWL*, p. 231
8. *SS*, p. 6

Air
1. *CGB*, p. 29
2. *SJ*, p. 360
3. *DWL*, p. 66
4. *SS*, p. 16
5. *TTW*, p. 314

Fire
1. *SJ*, p. 324
2. *TTW*, p. 73

3. *TTW,* p. 311
4. *SJ,* p. 252
5. *LL,* p. 31
6. *ES,* p. 375
7. *SS,* p. 25
8. *SS,* p. 174

Water
1. *SS,* p. 37
2. *SS,* p. 164
3. *VC,* p. 32
4. *OSM,* p. 100

Chapter 4 Firmament
Sky and Clouds
1. *TTW,* pp. 108-109
2. *SJ,* p. 340
3. *SJ,* p. 263
4. *SJ,* p. 243
5. *VC,* p. 72
6. *OSM,* p. 156
7. *DWL,* p. 158
8. *LL,* p. 18
9. *DWL,* p. 169
10. *DWL,* p. 5
11. *SSM,* pp. 30-31
12. *SJ,* p. 253
13. *ES,* p. 248
14. *ES,* p. 364
15. *OSM,* p. 98

Sun and Moon
1. *SJ,* p. 188
2. *CGB,* p. 179
3. *VC,* p. 65
4. *SJ,* p. 51
5. *ES,* p. 206
6. *VC,* p. 96
7. *DWL,* p. 232
8. *OSM,* p. 3
9. *OSM,* p. 47
10. *OSM,* p. 157

Planets and Stars
1. *DWL,* pp. 312-313
2. *TTW,* p. 291
3. *VC,* p. 92
4. *DWL,* p. 180
5. *OSM,* p. 55
6. *OSM,* p. 33
7. *OSM,* pp. 54-55
8. *DWL,* p. 14
9. *LL,* p. 30
10. *LL,* p. 19
11. *OSM,* p. 46
12. *DWL,* p. 177
13. *ES,* p. 417
14."Hagia Sophia," *ESF,* pp. 68-69

Chapter 5 Creatures
Butterflies and Birds
1. *DWL,* p. 123
2. *AJTM,* p. 107
3. *RTM,* p. 319
4. *SJ,* pp. 274-275
5. *CGB,* p. 140
6. *CGB,* p. 16
7. *CGB,* p. 23
8. *AJTM,* p. 223
9. *CGB,* p. 246
10. *SJ,* p. 292
11. *TTW,* p. 228
12. *OSM,* p. 100
13. *OSM,* p. 99
14. *DWL,* p. 245
15. *VC,* p. 185
16. *DWL,* p. 11
17. *DWL,* p. 162
18. *OSM,* p. 107
19. *TTW,* p. 332
20. *SS,* p. 202
21. *SS,* p. 202
22. *SS,* pp. 123-124
23. *TTW,* p. 186

24. *TTW,* p. 222
25. *TTW,* p. 342
26. *TTW,* p. 315
27. *VC,* p. 93
28. *DWL,* p. 313
29. *OSM,* p. 105

Rams and Lambs
1. *SJ,* p. 106
2. *ES,* p. 325
3. *OSM,* p. 98

Rodents and Rabbits
1. *DWL,* p. 308
2. *LL,* p. 10
3. *LL,* p. 168
4. *TTW,* p. 342
5. *VC,* p. 93
6. *ES,* pp. 203-204

Horses and Cattle
1. *CGB,* p. 304
2. *ES,* p. 363
3. *DWL,* p. 148
4. *ES,* p. 473
5. *TTW,* p. 128

Snakes and Frogs
1. *OSM,* p. 108
2. *OSM,* p. 68
3. *TTW,* p. 7
4. *DWL,* pp. 255-256
5. *ES,* p. 364
6. *OSM,* p. 64

Deer and Dogs
1. *LL,* p. 25
2. *DWL,* p. 180
3. *DWL,* p. 291
4. *DWL,* p. 271
5. *DWL,* p. 217
6. *DWL,* p. 189
7. *LL,* p. 208
8. *DWL,* pp. 315-316

9. *RTM,* p. 274
10. *RTM,* p. 362
11. *RTM,* p. 319

Bees and Bugs
1. *OSM,* p. 80
2. *RTM,* p. 355
3. *RTM,* pp. 347-348
4. *ES,* p. 332
5. *OSM,* p. 284
6. *TTW,* p. 51
7. *TTW,* p. 335
8. *TTW,* p. 335
9. *SS,* p. 93

Chapter 6 Festivals
Rain
1. "Rain and the Rhinoceros," *RU,* p. 13
2. *ES,* p. 325
3. *TTW,* p. 295
4. *TTW,* p. 108
5. "Rain and the Rhinoceros," *RU,* p. 9
6. *RTM,* p. 139
7. "Rain and the Rhinoceros," *RU,* p. 9
8. *SS,* pp. 135-136
9. *DWL,* p. 29
10. *LL,* p. 3
11. "Rain and the Rhinoceros," *RU,* p. 10
12. *TTW,* p. 116
13. *TTW,* p. 220
14. *NMI,* p. 254
15. *SJ,* p. 58
16. *DWL,* pp. 313-314
17. *VC,* p. 207
18. *OSM,* p. 81
19. *DWL,* p. 109
20. *OSM,* p. 23

21. "Rain and the Rhinoceros," *RU*,
    p. 10
22. "Rain and the Rhinoceros," *RU*,
    p. 23

Flowers
1. *TTW*, p. 227
2. *LL*, p. 202
3. *TTW*, p. 145
4. *SJ*, p. 71
5. *LL*, p. 202
6. *TTW*, p. 128
7. *TTW*, p. 16
8. *SJ*, p. 49
9. *OSM*, p. 99
10. *SS*, pp. 164-165

Trees
1. *SS*, p. 191
2. *OSM*, p. 97
3. *RTM*, p. 362
4. *SS*, p. 51
5. *OSM*, p. 112
6. *SS*, p. 45
7. *SS*, p. 93
8. *SS*, p. 233
9. *OSM*, p. 112
10. *SS*, p. 77

Chapter 7 Presences

Mountains
1. *SSM*, p. 11
2. "On the Anniversary of My
   Baptism," *CPTM*, p. 156
3. *ES*, p. 219
4. *OSM*, p. 94
5. *OSM*, p. 94
6. *OSM*, p. 94
7. *OSM*, pp. 195-196
8. *OSM*, p. 96
9. *OSM*, p. 100
10. *OSM*, p. 103
11. *OSM*, p. 106

12. *OSM*, p. 182
13. *OSM*, p. 187
14. *CGB*, pp. 188-189
15. *OSM*, pp. 189-190
16. *OSM*, p. 226
17. *OSM*, p. 237
18. *OSM*, p. 237
19. *OSM*, p. 284
20. *OSM*, p. 284
21. *OSM*, p. 284
22. *OSM*, p. 286
23. *OSM*, p. 290

Chapter 8 Sanctuary

Forest
1. *SS*, p. 232
2. *SS*, p. 16
3. *SS*, p. 292
4. *SSM*, p. 49
5. *LL*, p. 23
6. *ES*, pp. 328-331
7. *LL*, p. 208
8. *DWL*, pp. 239-242
9. *TTW*, p. 122
10. *LL*, p. 342

BIBLIOGRAPHY

The Journals of Thomas Merton. Patrick Hart, osco, general editor:

Volume One: 1939–1941, *Run to the Mountain: The Story of a Vocation.* Patrick Hart, osco, ed. San Francisco: HarperSanFrancisco, 1995.

Volume Two: 1941–1952, *Entering the Silence: Becoming a Monk and Writer.* Jonathan Montaldo, ed. San Francisco: HarperSanFrancisco, 1996.

Volume Three: 1952–1960, *A Search for Solitude: Pursuing the Monk's True Life.* Lawrence S. Cunningham, ed. San Francisco: HarperSanFrancisco, 1996.

Volume Four: 1960–1963, *Turning Toward the World: The Pivotal Years.* Victor A. Kramer, ed. San Francisco: HarperSanFrancisco, 1996.

Volume Five: 1963–1965, *Dancing in the Water of Life: Seeking Peace in the Hermitage.* Robert E. Daggy, ed. San Francisco: HarperSanFrancisco, 1997.

Volume Six: 1966–1967, *Learning to Love: Exploring Solitude and Freedom.* Christine M. Bochen, ed. San Francisco: HarperSanFrancisco, 1997.

Volume Seven: 1967–1968, *The Other Side of the Mountain: The End of the Journey.* Patrick Hart, osco, ed. San Francisco: HarperSanFrancisco, 1998.

Other Merton Journals

The Asian Journal of Thomas Merton, edited from his original notebooks by Naomi Burton, Patrick Hart, and James Laughlin. New York: New Directions Publishing Corp., 1973.

A Vow of Conversation: Journals 1964–1965, edited and with a preface by Naomi Burton Stone. New York: Farrar, Straus, Giroux, 1988.

Books by Thomas Merton

The Collected Poems of Thomas Merton, New York: New Directions, 1977.

Conjectures of a Guilty Bystander, 1st ed. Garden City, NY: Doubleday, 1966.

Emblems of a Season of Fury. Norfolk, CT: J. Laughlin, 1963.

"Honorable Reader": Reflections on My Work, edited by Robert E. Daggy. New York: Crossroad, 1989.

New Seeds of Contemplation. Norfolk, CT: New Directions, 1961.

No Man Is an Island. New York: Harcourt, Brace, 1955.

Raids on the Unspeakable. New York: New Directions, 1966.

The Seven Storey Mountain. New York: Harcourt, Brace, 1948.

The Sign of Jonas. New York: Harcourt, Brace, 1953.

ACKNOWLEDGMENTS

A Search for Solitude: The Journals of Thomas Merton, Volume Three 1952–1960 by Thomas Merton and edited by Lawrence S. Cunningham. Copyright © 1996 by The Merton Legacy Trust. Reprinted by permission of HarperCollins Publishers, Inc.

Turning Toward the World: The Journals of Thomas Merton, Volume Four 1960–1963 by Thomas Merton and edited by Victor A. Kramer. Copyright © 1996 by The Merton Legacy Trust. Reprinted by permission of HarperCollins Publishers, Inc.

Dancing in the Water of Life: The Journals of Thomas Merton, Volume Five 1963–1965 by Thomas Merton and edited by Robert E. Daggy. Copyright © 1997 by The Merton Legacy Trust. Reprinted by permission of HarperCollins Publishers, Inc.

Learning to Love: The Journals of Thomas Merton, Volume Six 1966–1967 by Thomas Merton and Edited by Christine Bochen. Copyright © 1997 by The Merton Legacy Trust. Reprinted by permission of HarperCollins Publishers, Inc.

The Other Side of the Mountain: The Journals of Thomas Merton, Volume Seven 1967–1968 by Thomas Merton and edited by Patrick Hart. Copyright © 1998 by The Merton Legacy Trust. Reprinted by permission of HarperCollins Publishers, Inc.

The Asian Journals of Thomas Merton, Copyright © 1975 by The Trustees of the Merton Legacy Trust, used by permission of New Directions Publishing Corporation.

The Collected Poems of Thomas Merton, copyright © 1977 by The Trustees of the Merton Legacy Trust, used by permission of New Directions Publishing Corporation.

New Seeds of Contemplation, Copyright © 1961 by The Abbey of Gethsemani, Inc., used by permission of New Directions Publishing Corporation.

No Man Is an Island by Thomas Merton, copyright © 1955 by The Abbey of Our Lady of Gethsemani and renewed 1983 by the Trustees of the Merton Legacy Trust, reprinted by permission of Harcourt, Inc.

The Seven Storey Mountain by Thomas Merton, copyright © 1948 by Harcourt, Inc., and renewed 1976 by the Trustees of the Merton Legacy Trust, reprinted by permission of the publisher.

The Sign of Jonas by Thomas Merton, copyright © 1953 by The Abbey of Our Lady of Gethsemani and renewed 1981 by the Trustees of the Merton Legacy Trust, reprinted by permission of Harcourt, Inc.

Looking for more?

The Contemplative Heart
James Finley
A former student of Thomas Merton at the Abbey of Gethsemani, James Finley shares the mystery and beauty of contemplative traditions and practices, unlocking the profound possibilities it has to offer all of us in our everyday lives.
ISBN: 1-893732-10-X / $13.95

Merton's Palace of Nowhere
James Finley
James Finley mines another rich vein of Merton's thought—the search for spiritual identity. A guide to the difficult journey to a realization of the true self.
ISBN: 0-87793-159-3 / $8.95

Earth's Echo
Sacred Encounters With Nature
Robert M. Hamma
Leads readers to reflect on the sacred reality of nature as found in different settings: the seashore, the river, the forest, the desert, and the mountains.
ISBN: 1-893732-46-0 / $12.95

Prices subject to change.